I0141150

The Five Basic Principles For Life

Lifetime Fundamentals

By Michael Carroll, Jr.

Success is a journey, not a destination – Ben Sweetland

He who gets wisdom loves his own soul; he who cherishes understanding prospers Proverbs 19:8 (NIV)

Published by
Carroll Partners, LLC
4 Daniels Farm Rd
Suite 320
Trumbull, CT 06611

Copyright 2012 by Carroll Partners
All Right Reserved

ISBN ISBN-10: 0985364092
ISBN-13: 978-0-9853640-9-0

THE HOLY BIBLE, NEW INTERNATIONAL VERSION®, NIV® Copyright ©
1973, 1978, 1984, 2011 by Biblica, Inc.™ Used by permission. All rights
reserved worldwide.

Scripture quotations marked (NLT) are taken from the Holy Bible, New
Living Translation, copyright © 1996, 2004, 2007 by Tyndale House
Foundation. Used by permission of Tyndale House Publishers, Inc.,
Carol Stream, Illinois 60188. All rights reserved.

Scripture taken from the New King James Version. Copyright © 1982 by
Thomas Nelson, Inc. Used by permission. All rights reserved.

Scripture taken from The Message. Copyright © 1993, 1994, 1995,
1996, 2000, 2001, 2002. Used by permission of NavPress Publishing
Group.

©2012 by Carroll Partners, LLC
All rights reserved.
Printed in the United States of America

- - - -

The program developed on these pages is the direct result of the leadership, guidance and inspiration of the Father, Son and Holy Spirit to bring freedom to all people, regardless of spiritual beliefs, from the burdens of society. Only when one is truly free can they experience real success.

- - - -

Table of Contents

The Principle of Success

Success is a journey, not a destination – Ben Sweetland

He who gets wisdom loves his own soul; he who cherishes understanding prospers Proverbs 19:8 (NIV)

We learn to walk by the time we are one; we learn to ride a bike by the time we're six, about the same time we are starting school. We learn to drive by the time we are sixteen. We get married, have kids and then retire. We do this, most of us anyway, without learning about success. I'm talking about real success. Some of us may have learned society's version of success and that is precisely why we are unhappy and unfulfilled. Of true success, we know very little or even nothing. Many of us never learn what success is and what it isn't. We don't understand what failure is or what it isn't.

If you look around at the world today you will see many people leading unfulfilled, unhappy and unproductive lives. No one ever taught us about success. There are no high school courses on the subject and I have yet to see a college course that teaches life-long principles that, if lived by, will set your destiny in a new trajectory. Well, that's what this program is about. By going through this program and learning to practice this principle alongside the other Principles, you will begin to uncover the life that was meant for *you*. You will realize your uniqueness and finally realize that we are not living in a one-size-fits-all world. You will uncover true happiness as you begin to realize success.

As we begin our journey, I would like to share with you my personal experiences with *success* as the world and popular society defines it and what I have come to know as true, lasting and real success. My journey began, like everyone else, as a child. It's when we are young and impressionable that our beliefs, attitudes and behaviors are formed. They affect the rest of our lives, and for many people, it is never realized that they may develop these characteristics in an atmosphere that isn't or wasn't supportive of real success.

My first experiences with worldly success revolved around sports and money. These two areas were given major emphasis. As I remember I was strongly persuaded to practice baseball everyday and I also had a paper route. I remember hearing from people who had an influence on my life that I could do anything and have as much money as I wanted. Wow, what's wrong with that? So the race was on. Like many young people, my ambitions began to revolve around power, importance, prestige and money. The cues from society, in general, were the same. I should want "stuff" and I should do whatever it takes to get that "stuff." That was *success*!

I took a job as an insurance and investment broker out of college, after seeing the movie "Wall Street." I felt important and there was some feeling of power. After all, I was helping people with their money. There was some feeling of prestige, especially among friends and people who didn't know the industry that well. I didn't make much money though and found out later why. It was not what I was supposed to do. In an industry where they hire almost anybody who walks through the door, I wasn't making the money I thought I deserved. I came to realize years later, that I wasn't working nearly as intelligently or efficiently as I needed to in order to make that money. I would work twelve to sixteen hours a day; I realize now that I was sitting at a desk for twelve to sixteen hours a day, but not really working.

When I met my wife, I remember telling her with an absolute degree of certainty that I was going to be the richest man in the world; I was going to be successful. I don't know if she bought into that or not, but she married me anyway. I think that I might have convinced her somewhere along the way, if she wasn't already convinced. So off we went chasing *success*. After some time of this we figured out what we thought the real problem was, it was the insurance and investment industry. So, I quit my job and took other sales jobs, working equally tiring hours; driving both of us insane with no time for fun or leisure.

I don't think it was until our son came along in 2004 that we realized what we were doing to ourselves. We were working and expending energy toward goals and ideals that were not our own. So what did we do? We quit our jobs. We would be successful on our own, without the help of anyone else. We went and bought some computers, desks, chairs and a two-line phone and went into business for ourselves. Doing what? Well, selling insurance and investments of course. Needless to say, we were not "successful," but we kept up the chase. I don't think it was until we had our daughter in 2007 that we realized what we were doing.

Now I have always been happy with my wife, she is my best friend and business partner. I have the two best kids anyone could have asked or hoped for but I couldn't figure out why I couldn't make any money. Why I couldn't be "successful." I could run 4 miles and work out everyday. I could eat fairly good food; have energy and health. I could have great relationships with my wife and kids, but I couldn't be "successful". As could be anticipated, I was very frustrated. Then, through a series of financial disasters and failures, our eyes began to open. We were *successful*. This program will help to show you how we did it.

We began to realize that we were chasing the world's concept of *success*. We were told what the world thought success was and we pursued it, not realizing that we didn't want it. Being in charge of the world's money supply wasn't in the cards for us. Thank God!

I never realized that I was successful and that I had been for a very long time. I was chasing an idea of success that wasn't mine. Yes, I owned it by the ideas, beliefs and attitudes that I had learned in my childhood and was reinforced in my teenage and early adult years, but I continued to own it for much of my life just because I was not aware of the truth.

When I began to look around, I saw that I had a strong relationship with my Creator. I had the love, friendship and trust of my wife. I had the respect and love of my kids. I had my health and intelligence. I had so many positives in my life, even in spite of the difficulties but I was deceived into thinking that I wasn't worth very much. I now know that I am successful not only because I have all of the things that were mentioned above, but also because of the value and worth I bring to others lives. I don't mean monetary value but the positive comment in the midst of a negative atmosphere. They are the words of encouragement to someone who is feeling down or left out. It's having the conviction to stand my ground on what I believe to be true or right no matter what the consequences. Maybe yes, I have been successful for most of my life.

It's time for you to take a look at your own life. Who defines whether you are successful or not? We all are social creations. We all strive at some level to be accepted. That feeling of acceptance is what many people seek as their measure of success. If people around us are praising us then we must be doing well! So at this point we need to be honest (honesty is a key to success in this program) with ourselves. Friends, family, co-workers or business partners and the expectations of society have determined success in general for most people. It's hard to admit, but it's true, if you examine the things you have been striving for, you are sure to find many of the people who fall into the groups mentioned above have shaped you and your definition of success. But who should define success in your life?

I am going to go out on a limb here; I am suggesting that success should be defined by God and by your relationship with Him. I know that I turned some people off with that statement but I ask you to remember, back in the introduction, where I asked you to suspend all fear, doubt and disbelief. Did you mean it? Are you willing to continue with the program? If what I have to say isn't true, real and relevant to you by the time you complete this program then you can disregard what I say and just go back to your old ways.

Yes, your definition of success should be based on God! It has been said "He who pursues righteousness and love finds life, prosperity and honor."[1] In other words, if you are doing the right things for the right reasons, you *will* be successful.

We are taught at an early age that if we try hard enough we can be whatever we want. I do believe this, to a certain extent, but it misses the point of real success. Yes, if I spend my life working 14 hours a day, 7 days a week staying on top of all the financial journals and magazines, neglecting my wife and kids, forgoing real opportunities to do good in society and to help others then there is a very real possibility that I can be a successful insurance and investment broker. I can make a ton of money, but I would be miserable and so would everyone around me. I would add no real value to the world. I would just be a slave to what I think success is.

Take the example of someone who, without a God given athletic ability, sets out to play basketball in the NBA. He has been told that he can be anything he wants if he sets his mind to it. So he goes out in pursuit of his "dream." He spends his day practicing, giving up opportunities to meet new people, and add value to other people's lives. He may even make it into professional basketball but because that isn't what he was meant to do, there is a tremendous amount of unhappiness. He feels unfulfilled and begins to spend his money on frivolous things. To fill the void in his life he begins experimenting with drugs. He ends up bankrupt and in a rehab somewhere wondering how it happened. Sound extreme? I don't think so! This story is being played out everyday in every sport, in Hollywood and in every other industry. The same thing happens to us even though we are not in the public spotlight. When we give everything we have and push for something we aren't supposed to do we end up bankrupt: spiritually, emotionally, socially and financially.

By allowing your relationship with God to form the basis of your pursuits and aspirations, you are tapping into a source of unlimited power and potential. Yes, YOU WERE CREATED FOR SOMETHING! By pursuing the reasons for your existence you will be more successful than you ever dreamed possible. Success should flow in your life, not be a constant struggle. Yes, there are setbacks and difficult times along the way, but the overall direction of your life and pursuits will all make sense and fall into a pattern of actions, which despite all of the circumstances around you, will move you forward in pursuit of that childhood dream or vision that you had for your life before it was distorted by worldly thinking and influence.

I am not saying that you will have a "free ride" and that your life will be effortless when you find your true purpose and begin to fulfill it, but I will tell you that you will have a sense of peace, serenity and confidence in the face of calamity. You will develop a sense of faith to see you through the hard times and a sense of humility to see you through the easy times.

You will learn to take the next right action in your life and you will begin to see how these tiny actions in your life string together to create success in *every* area of your life.

The victory has already been won. All you need to do is look at the choices you are presented with and make the right ones. Choices as small as holding the door open for the person behind you at the mall or making a phone call in the next 5 minutes to speak to someone who you have been putting off. It doesn't matter what "compartment" the next right action is in, take it in the moment and God will lead you along the path of success. You will enjoy peace and prosperity like never before. Will you give it a try?

Destroy Your Profit Motive

It has been said, "Do not wear yourself out to get rich; have the wisdom to show restraint."[2] I think this truth has been lost in the world today. People run around trying to accumulate things. They work long hours in an effort to get more stuff. They sacrifice time spent with family and friends to feel *successful*. What is the fruit of all this materialism? Everywhere marriages are falling apart; children who never get the benefit of a relationship with their parents, and emptiness and despair as people reach for more of everything.

If your only motivation for trying this program is to make more money and accumulate more stuff, you need to make some hard choices. Is that what you *really* want? Is something telling you that there is more than what you are currently seeking? Will more money and stuff really make you happy? You already know the answers to these questions.

The irony to all of this is, that once you stop the full-on pursuit of money and material possessions, once you begin to practice the rest of the principles in this program, and once you move money down to the bottom of your list of priorities, you will begin to experience *true* wealth, abundance and success. It is here that money will begin to flow into your life. Yes, you will have to put in an honest effort and a fair days work, but that's all you need to do. The rest just happens.

Also, learn to do things without the thought of getting anything back. Volunteer your time, energy and talents to make the lives of everyone you know better. By doing this, you are teaching your brain that there is more than enough time, energy and talents to go around. Your faith will grow and you will know that you have abundance in all areas of your life. I am reminded of an experience Danielle and I had years ago, in 2002. We were sitting outside of a KB Toy Store about four weeks before Christmas. I remember it was snowing and cold. This particular year we had a very hard time financially. I had lost my job over the summer and had not been able to find any work. We had recently bought our house and gotten married. We were discussing whether we were going to go in the toy store to do our yearly shopping for Toys-for-Tots. We had donated to this organization every year since we had known each other. This year was different though; we only had half of our household income coming in each month. We were falling short on our bills and were using our savings to cover the difference. We were both nervous about the finances, but our hearts told us to give. How would we do it since we had no extra money? I'll tell you what we did. We drained our savings account and used that money for the toys. Want to know something? We were okay. We were better than okay. God made sure of it. That following January is when Carroll Partners, LLC was founded (The parent company to Family Coaching Central). In spite of the struggles since the night of that all-important decision, God has ALWAYS taken care of us in our abundance. To be honest with you, there have been *many* times when we have come right down to the moment when we needed Him and He has yet to let us down. So we keep right on going. We give of our time, talents, energy and money without the thought of getting anything back.

In Order to Experience Real Success, You Must First Be A Big Failure

I know many people will scoff at the above words, but they are true. The kind of real success that I am talking about in this program is much more than society's version of success, i.e. a big house, a fancy car and a wad of money. Funny thing is that I happen to know people like that, we all do. Many times those people are not successful because there is no sense of fulfillment and not much to life beyond their career and quest for money. There is the crowd who went to college, got a good job and has been climbing the corporate ladder, never looking back. I am really happy for those types, if they want me to be, but I'm appealing to someone else here.

I am talking to the man or woman who has failed and failed big! Maybe you took a chance on business and lost, you lost all financial security and many possessions. I am talking to the one who may have had relationships shattered or dreams fail. The one who has experienced overwhelming heartbreak and pain. You may have allowed your health to deteriorate to the point where you don't think you can recover. There are an *infinite* number of possible places you have failed in your life. Some of us have had that experience in more than one area of our life. Maybe your whole life has been one miserable failure after another.

Maybe you have lost heart; you can't find the courage, strength, energy or faith to continue. You may feel that you have hit a dead end in life. This, you believe, is how you will finish up your miserable existence. I have good news for you, if you will listen. You are in a great place. You have a chance to experience success on a level you didn't even think was possible. The reason? You can appreciate it. You know where you've been so the success you gain by following this and the other principles in the program will allow you to let that appreciation shine through in everything you do. You will appreciate when things are going well and you will appreciate the challenges, troubles and hardships that lead to personal, emotional and spiritual growth. You will understand the words: "I know what it is to be in need, and I know what it is to have plenty. I have learned the secret of being content in any and every situation, whether well fed or hungry, whether living in plenty or in want."[3] When you have failed you have taken the first step towards success.

The One Who Failed Most of the Time

People who succeed know one important fact; In order to get to success, they must experience failure on a massive scale. For anyone who has read self-help or motivational books, I will not go through the pains of boring you about the countless Hall of Fame baseball players who have failed over 75% of the time (and these guys are the best at what they do). You are probably not a professional baseball player, nor is it likely that you are trying to secure a spot for yourself in the Hall of Fame (if you are, keep reading, this program can help you too). The point is, that the best of the best know this "secret."

Is it possible to live up to your potential and experience real success without failure? I haven't met anyone yet who has done this. There are people living in their comfort zones and are not experiencing failure, but these people are selling themselves short. It's only when you're out there, taking chances and testing your limits, that you will learn valuable lessons and experience the spiritual growth necessary for real success.

The pain of failure causes you to look inward rather than outward. This usually occurs when the pain of failure has become more unbearable than the pain of growing. Sounds painful, huh? It's not that bad when you learn to recognize that the pain of growing will lead you to better things. You begin to embrace that pain and you often begin to seek it out because it leads to a better life. Besides, once you do begin the journey into real success and begin to experience it, the joy, peace, serenity, fun and feelings of accomplishment far outweigh any pain you may experience. It's only when you decide to stand still in life and feel sorry for yourself that the pain becomes excruciating. Take the lessons that you have learned in life and apply them to *your* situation. I don't know what they are for you, but I know that you have them. I read a book recently and I would recommend it to everyone. The name of the book is "Think and Grow Rich," by Napoleon Hill. In this book the author talks about "the seed of an equivalent benefit." Use your failures and pains to grow. It is about finding the lesson to be learned in *every* circumstance and every situation. Even when Thomas Edison was trying to create the light bulb, he failed many times. When asked about these failures, he replied, "I have not failed. I've just found 10,000 ways that won't work."

The good news now, is that you can improve, grow and begin to experience real success without always experiencing pain. If you take this advice and apply it in your life, then your eyes have been opened. You are no longer living in ignorance about your own state of affairs. If you have let your exercise program slip over the last several years you can begin again, today, before the doctor tells you that you need to. If you have been neglecting family or friends because of hectic work schedules, you can leave early today to spend some extra time with those you love, before your kids are grown and the opportunity is lost. If you have been neglecting taking time for yourself, take a quiet walk in the park before the stress of everyday life forces an ailment on you that makes you take a sick day. The point is to do something you want to before you have to do something you don't want to.

See Action Step #1

What Success Isn't: The First Point in Understanding Success

Before defining what real success is for our purpose in this program and hopefully for you as you move forward, it is important to discover what success is not. The world and our troubled society have had a lot to do with most people's current definition of success. If you were to take a field trip to your local mall and stand at one of the entrances, you would get a fair cross section of society. If you asked each person who walked by you to *define* success in their life, you would get many different answers. The answers would be just as varied as the people who pass by. I would be willing to bet, though, that the vast majority of these answers would revolve around the following themes: power, prestige, fame and the big ones, money and possessions.

None of these things bring success in one's life. The first three have nothing to do with real success and probably do a lot more to destroy someone, rather than build them up into who they need to become in order to achieve this elusive animal called success. The other two, money and possessions, definitely play a *part* in the overall picture of one's success, but it is just a *part*.

Let's settle this here and now! Yes, it is okay and even good to have money and possessions in your life. For most people though, it is the other way around, the money and things have them.

Let's look at the typical day for the average person and see where we, as a society, have lost focus on real success. We will use a guy I know. His name is Joe Average. He gets up around 6:30 am with the alarm going off and he probably hits the snooze bar several times; it's about 7:00 am when he finally gets up. He then realizes that he probably shouldn't have stayed up so late last night. He hurries out of the house to start his morning commute to his job that he dislikes or maybe even hates. He knows he should be doing something else with his life, but isn't sure what. He gets to work 5 minutes late and gets right into "making things happen." He is unfocussed and spends ten to twelve hours doing his work. He gets home around 7:00 pm, eats dinner, watches TV, or maybe even meets some friends at the local bar. He then gets to bed late again and starts the whole cycle all over. He does this because he feels he will be "successful" *someday*.

In the meantime, he has neglected the important things in life. He doesn't take care of his health, doesn't do much exercise and probably doesn't eat very well, therefore he lacks energy to have any real passion for living, working and yes, playing. His relationships are superficial, at best. Maybe he is "friends" with some people at work and they go to the bar several nights a week or they play on the company softball team, but the prospect of true friendship just doesn't occur to him. When he does get together with these people it is mostly an attempt to impress each other and to show the others how "together" his life is.

His home life is spent squabbling over such trivial stuff that his home life, where he should have a refuge from the world, has just become an extension of the rest of everything else. If there are kids, there is no real relationship being formed. They all might plop themselves in front of the TV several nights a week but there is no *REAL* interaction. As far as plans for the future and accomplishing something greater, well, those dreams died out a long time ago. Rather than living, our friend Joe has settled into a pattern of just existing.

There are so many stories like Mr. Average. The details are different, but the general outcomes are the same. Take Jane Average for example, the other half of the Average family. She does different things, has a different job and different "friends" but the outcome is the same; a feeling of despair and worry about where life is leading. How do I know this? That's where I was for most of my life. Fortunately, I discovered that things could be different, much different, and I have never been so fulfilled in my life. The first move in this direction will occur when you realize that the problem with worldly success is that we were all not created to be rich, powerful and famous. Success is not at some point in the future. It is here and now. The good news is that you can stop chasing the gold at the end of the rainbow; it isn't there. We were all created for a different role and a different experience. This is a good thing and you will begin to see that as you work through this program. In order to move forward, we must first figure out what success is. Start soon though because time is ticking and there are no do-overs.

See Action Step #2

<u>What Success is: The Starting Point</u>

Now that we know what success is not, how do we define what it is? Maybe what you always thought was true has now been turned upside down. That's okay. That's more than okay; you are now at the starting point of an incredible journey. One that may even take you places that you never dreamed you would go. You may even see some old childhood dreams re-emerge. One thing is for sure, if you stay on the path you have now begun, and work at it continually, you will have *real success*. Most of all have fun! Dale Carnegie once said, "People rarely succeed unless they have fun in what they are doing."

Dictionary.com defines success as: the attainment of wealth, position, honors, or the like.

I would like to define success differently. To me, success is constant improvement and movement toward a worthwhile purpose, while constantly raising the bar as you reach small achievements. At the same time, you will be enriching your and everybody else's life that you come in contact with. This definition sounds quite confusing, doesn't it? I can simplify it by saying: *Success is taking the next right action.* Let's take the latter definition rather than the former. They encompass the same thing, but remember I am seeking simplicity and so should you.

You must decide now how you will know when you have achieved success? Because of our worldly programming, most people feel successful by having one or more of the following things occur in their lives:

- Someone tells them they are successful.

- They have an internal feeling of success.

- They measure their achievements.

The first two of these are probably based on our past experience and most likely do not really reveal any success or failure on our part. Rather, they are more of a reflection of us doing what we have been taught by society. The third one can work one of two ways. If you have broken your achievements down sufficiently, then yes, you can use your measurements of achievement to see some success in your life but it does not measure *all* success.

The best way to measure success is to take an honest look at the "fruit" you are producing in your life. Some success if only measured by achievement, can be really discouraging. You may be in a position where you are really working hard to achieve a result in your life. You feel you are getting nowhere. The truth is that you are on the verge of a real breakthrough. Or you may have just been working on a project that may take years to complete. In these situations, it wouldn't be fair to yourself if you were measuring by results. Sometimes the results may be a long way off.

Many years ago I came across a short prayer that I believe encompasses all success. It is called the prayer of St. Francis and here it is:

"Lord, make me an instrument of Your peace.

Where there is hatred, let me sow love;

where there is injury, pardon;

where there is doubt, faith;

where there is despair, hope;

where there is darkness, light;

where there is sadness, joy.

O, Divine Master,

grant that I may not so much seek

to be consoled as to console;

to be understood as to understand;

to be loved as to love;

For it is in giving that we receive;

it is in pardoning that we are pardoned;

it is in dying that we are born again to eternal life.
Amen."

I remember when I rediscovered these words several years ago. I was introduced to this prayer as a child, but my mind and spirit were not ready to take hold of the truths that it reveals. Later, as I was doing research for this program, they popped off the computer screen as I was researching success. These words encompass what it means to take the next right action. They will lead to real success in *all* areas of your life.

Let's now examine briefly, the areas in which you should be seeking real success for your life. This list is meant as a guide only; you may add other areas to it, but most of the growth you are seeking in your life will fall under one of these categories. They are in no particular order and will be discussed throughout this program, so I will only list them here.

1. **Vision Success** - Are you doing what you were created to do?

2. **Financial/Material Success** - Figure out how much money you need and then figure out how to get that money.

3. **Family Success** - Your family should be a refuge from the world; a place where you build others up and support those you love most. Is it like that for you?

4. **Relationship Success** - Do you experience fulfilling relationships or are you stressed out with those you spend time with?

5. **Recreational Success** - Life should be fulfilling and fun. Is yours?

6. **Physical/Health Success** - How well you are able to practice this program all depends on how you feel.

7. **Spiritual Success** - The most important aspect for your existence is your relationship with God; it can always be improved.

As you gain real success in these areas, your life will become - satisfying, fulfilling and fun. All of these areas work together to create who you are as a whole person and you need to be focusing on *all* of them in order to make significant progress in *any* of them. For example, you cannot focus only on recreational success without doing any work on your financial matters. This will lead you to poverty. Also, you can't focus only on financial and material gain without working towards improving your relationships. This will lead to lack of fulfillment and loneliness. There are numerous examples and I have known many people who have tried to excel in one or two of these areas without working on them all. Trust me; the result has always been the same. Failure in all areas, even the one or one's they were concentrating on. Take control of your success now by improving your *whole* life.

What is Failure?

Failure is giving up. Failure is taking the lumps and pains that have come your way and crawling in a hole somewhere to feel sorry for yourself. Failure is a way for us to create excuses for not becoming who God wants us to be.

For much of my life I had always thought of failure in a negative way. I thought failure was this horrible monster that was to be avoided at any and all costs. Wow, was I wrong. I have learned that failure, if used properly is actually a stepping stone of success.

What Failure Isn't

As I previously discussed about what success is and is not, I think it is appropriate to have the same discussion about failure, before I move on. If you are to experience *any* success in life, then it is almost certain that you will experience setbacks along the way. In fact, the more success you have, the more "failure" you will encounter before, during and after that success. Remember this and keep it in front of you continually. Print it in big letters and keep it in front of you. Refer to it often.

Setbacks and losses are *not* failures! If you are working towards definite objectives and have a clear vision in your life; if you keep yourself "fit" in all areas of your life then you will have very little to worry about when this "monster," we all call failure, shows up.

By practicing this program, you will be able to move past failure and into a world full of success, filled with possibilities.

A great example of failure is the apostle Paul, before he actually became an apostle. He had everything that was important to the world. He had power, money and what he thought was happiness. Then one day he got knocked off his horse[4]. From there, to keep the story short, I will just tell you that he endured much "failure." The things that he encountered would have made most men or women give up and turn and run into their self made comfort zones. Not Paul, he just kept moving forward, in spite of the pain and setbacks. What he accomplished through all of that is success greater than any man on this earth. For those of you who don't know, Paul wrote the majority of the New Testament in the Bible (The number 1 book seller of all time).

What Permanent Failure Is

It is important to know the difference between permanent failure and temporary failure. Most people never make that distinction. They allow the normal setbacks, that are designed and allowed into our lives to push us along and make us grow, to become life altering and destroying events. They allow these things to sap their energy, and destroy their dreams. They allow bitterness and resentment into their lives.

Dictionary.com defines failure as: a subnormal quantity or quality; an insufficiency. These definitions center around a "lack of success." They are created by a troubled world that does not understand real success and the steps that are needed to create that success. For the purposes of this program and for your purposes, if you really want success in your life, you should understand what real failure is. Failure in life, the real and permanent failure that so many people experience on a regular basis, even as a way of life, is caused by giving up or not even starting in the first place. To make it simple, real failure is sin. You are taking this perfect creation (You) and not fulfilling your potential or destiny. Too many people believe that if they experience loss or setbacks then they are failures. That is the sad state of society today. However, you don't have to live with that belief any longer.

Hopefully you have already begun to ask yourself, "How do I overcome failure then?" Good question! There is a simple answer; *give yourself permission to fail!* One of the guiding beliefs that I have designed my life around is that it is impossible to fail. If I just continue to move forward, even if it's an inch at a time, I will *eventually* reach my destination. It is important to remember, that even if you move forward by an inch, there may be circumstances that put you back 10 feet! Just pick yourself up and start again. It has been said and very appropriately, that *"most of the important things in the world have been accomplished by people who have kept on trying when there seemed to be no hope at all"*[5]. That is true of this program, my life, and if you let it, your life too!

One final note on failure, do not pursue perfection! This is the surest path to a lifetime of frustration and real failure. You cannot achieve perfection! There are probably so many great ideas out there in people's minds, but because they want it to be "perfect" their projects never get off the ground. I am not saying that you should be sloppy or haphazard in your work; just don't wait until everything is perfect before you move forward, otherwise you may be waiting a long time.

The Problem With Traditional "Self-Help" Programs

I remember when I was really young, probably my early teens, I read an ad in a magazine about being able to do or be *anything* I wanted. So, like many other people, I decided to give it a shot. Guess what? It didn't work. I was out about twenty dollars, but even worse, my wallet was open. I pursued these programs, buying new ones as they came out. After all, once a publisher or distributor of "self-help" programs sells you one, you are then on their mailing list and you begin to receive catalogs describing how good things can be, if you only spend a little more money. Like most people, I spent a ton of money, but got nowhere.

"Self-help" programs do not work! They never have and never will. I am sure there's a small percentage of the population who have used these programs and have gotten results, but for most of us, the problem with traditional self-help programs is, you guessed it, they rely on "self." Remember, "self" is what got you into your current mess; "self" most certainly can't get you out. Stop relying on "self."

"Self-help" programs are created by "experts." My experience has been that experts have a way of taking the extremely simple and making it extremely complicated. Sit down with any accountant and discuss taxes with him for just a little while; you will be sorry that you did. Also, step into any gym and watch the personal trainers instructing people on how to exercise. It is the same in virtually *any* field. We humans have a way of doing that.

If a squirrel could talk, and you asked him how he was preparing for winter, he would tell you that he was going to build a nest and store some nuts. Ask a zoologist the same question and you'll get a 300-page textbook. All you need to do to find proof of this in the measurement of human success and happiness, is to look around you at all of the people seeing psychologists and therapists. There are more of these professionals than at any time in human history. At the same time, there are more unhappy people than ever before. They make problems where there are none in an attempt to be important and relevant. In fact, I believe that there are experts in almost every field, including the so called "self-help" experts who, in an attempt to sound intelligent or relevant, will make statements that are so *bizarre* and *outrageous* that others assume they are true. Don't rely on "experts!" I'm not saying you shouldn't take advice from others, you should. Seek people who are getting the results you want and listen to what they are doing. It is clear that you should "listen to advice and accept instructions, and in the end you will be wise."[6]

In other words, don't accept marriage advice from a relationship "expert" who has been divorced 10 times! Traditional "self-help" programs tell you that your success or failure in life, mostly referring to material possessions and money, is up to you and you *alone*. What these programs fail to acknowledge is that your "success" or "failure" is about far more than you - If you only work hard, if you only think positively, if you only fill in the blank. Yes, you need to work hard and think positive thoughts, in fact as Zig Ziglar puts it: "the most practical beautiful, workable philosophy in the world won't work if you won't." Ultimately, your success or failure is far beyond you. Remember, most of the problems in the world are caused by self-reliance. Self-reliance causes your pride and ego to kick into overdrive. Self-reliance causes fear to bubble up to the surface because deep inside of you there is a realization that you aren't capable and need something *bigger* than yourself.

I propose something different. I know it may be difficult, but learn to rely on something bigger than you. I am not saying that it doesn't depend on you at all; I am simply saying that your success or failure depends a lot less on you than you ever thought or were led to believe and a lot more on forces outside of your control. Yes, you need to do the leg-work and supply the willingness, which we will discuss in much more detail later in the program, but for now you just need to stop relying only on yourself!

Most of the traditional "self-help" programs I have seen and tried myself are based on greed and selfishness. You are told that if you follow the prescribed program, at some point in the future a big house, a new car and a suitcase full of money will fall out of the sky, land right in front of you and BAM you'll be happy! They play into our fears and greed. We think these things fill the voids in our lives and they do, temporarily, until we are no longer satisfied and we want more. These programs talk very little of real and lasting success.

Self-help programs just don't work. Yes, you can improve by carefully selecting and implementing a self-help program. What I have found though, is the improvements are usually temporary and most people return to their old behaviors shortly after trying the program. The reason is because most of these programs focus only on the surface stuff. They don't dig deep into a person's character to uncover and fix the character issues that are holding them back from achieving their full potential. If you are trying this program I am sure that this is probably not your first attempt at trying to improve yourself or become "successful." If you follow *this* program and continually work at it, this will be the last program that you will ever need. Give yourself permission to try as you go through this program and you will be amazed at the results. This program works!

It's important to realize that this program is *not* "self-help!" You must admit here and now, that up to the point where you started this program, your self-run life was not really working out the best that it could. You may have been "surviving" or "getting by" but as for real success you have not really seen too much. Without that first admission and initial honesty, you may as well give this program away to someone else.

"Self-help" programs simply do not work for real and lasting results in your life. I said this before, I researched many "self-help" programs and admit that there are many good insights and lessons that can be taken and learned from some of these programs. In this program, I did the research for you.

We sorted through the good and the bad, the great and the horribly bad lessons and advice. The information and advice that is worth applying in your life is in *this* program.

Self is what got you into your current circumstances and situations. While they are not all bad, you must first admit and realize what brought you to the starting point of this program. Now is the time to really begin leaning on something bigger than yourself. You will be doing things along the way to make your life better and you more successful, but you are not the cause of any success you may enjoy. It is God! (Remember, that at the start of this program you agreed to suspend your fear, doubt and disbelief?) When you first realize this and then accept it, you will see how you receive guidance and direction, but you take the actual steps. If you *do* believe, then there is no convincing needed. I simply ask that for the duration of this program you place your trust in Him and allow good things to follow.

This program, if followed and acted upon, will have a tremendous impact on your life and for many people, it will introduce them to real success. Before I talk about all of the positives, let's take a moment to discuss what the program will *not* do. There are many people looking for a "quick-fix" for all of life's problems. This program is not that "quick-fix." There is hard work ahead for you if you expect to achieve real success in your life. Yes, it's worth it! You will not lose 300 pounds in the next seven days, nor will you become a billionaire in the next thirty. Your life will not become problem free nor will you make all of your relationships stronger than ever before, when you wake up tomorrow. You will not be an Olympic athlete in the next 6 weeks; you will not move your family into a mansion on the beach in two weeks and buy the yacht you always thought you deserved in three weeks.

So *what* will this program do? It will give you more than you ever dreamed possible. I talk to many people who are not even clear about *what* they want. This program will help you clarify what is really important. Most of the time what you thought you really wanted is nothing in comparison to the plans God has for you and your life. Yes, you *will* gain material objects such as a new house and more money. Your relationships *will* get better; your health *will* improve and the list goes on and on. It's safe to say that every area of your life that is worth improving, will improve. However, it's important to remember that it will take time and patience.

You will have direction and guidance. Your priorities will change and so will your goals and dreams (if they have been misdirected up to this point). I can only tell you from experience, that my life is nothing like I thought it would be, and my life is *better* than I could have ever dreamed possible.

Until creating this program and living by the principles set forth, I had no idea how good things could get. In spite of the difficulties and hardships, things are GOOD! They can be for you too. Are you ready? It has been said that, "whoever accepts guidance and seeks God will be blessed."[7] If you are doubting this statement, just give it a try and you will see that it is true.

The best thing you will gain from this program is "the peace that passes all understanding"[8] You will have peace and serenity in your life *regardless* of what is happening around you. Many programs out there claim that if you only do what they say, you will have no problems or challenges and life will be perfect. If that is what you are aiming for in life, then you don't understand real success. Real success is moving forward, in spite of difficulties. Although you will still have problems and difficulties, even if you work this program perfectly, (which is impossible), I can tell you that your problems, difficulties and challenges will change. As you conquer your present ones, you will grow. As you grow, you will be presented with new problems, difficulties and challenges. Through all of this, if you maintain your focus on this program and your desire to grow, you will maintain peace and serenity in your life. This will spread to everyone around you and you will be a force for positive and good in other people's lives, as well as your own.

Things To Remember While Pursuing Real Success

There are several things I ask you to keep in mind as you are learning to grasp this new concept of success. These tips will help you to *thoroughly* evaluate where you stand with regards to real success in your life. Some of them have been mentioned already and all of them will be mentioned again throughout this program.

The first thing to remember is that "experts" complicate things. This is not to say that you shouldn't seek help or ask for guidance when you need it. I think seeking advice is very important. "Plans are established by seeking advice..."[9] I *am* saying you should ask people who are getting the results you are seeking. Don't ask someone simply because they are an "expert." Also, don't avoid asking someone, simply because they are not formally educated on a topic. I remember when I used to pay hundreds of dollars to have the brakes done on my car. The mechanic would make the procedure sound difficult and complicated. Then one day, without enough money to get a much needed brake job, I decided to do some research. What I found was how amazingly simple doing a brake job is. If you can change a tire you can fix your brakes.[10] I have since saved thousands of dollars because I stopped relying on "the experts."

T.D. Jakes has said: "Success can be as painful as failure if you are not equipped for it." You must be *ready* for it. When success comes, usually after a season of long struggles, it comes fast. Don't allow it to overwhelm you. Make sure that you are prepared. The best way you can do that is to make sure you are constantly practicing all of the fundamentals in this program. You will make mistakes in practicing these principles, but after each mistake be sure that you get up and continue to move forward.

Remember that success and achievement are different. In many cases they do go together and complement each other. They also may be independent of each other in certain circumstances. You may go to the gym everyday to work on your physical health (success) but you haven't set a goal to run a triathlon or a marathon (achievement). As you can see from the above example, they can go together. Obviously if you are training for a marathon you will be healthy but you don't have to run a marathon in order to be successful at improving your health. The Principle of Achievement, part of this program, will be discussed at a later time. Right now it's important for you to focus on real success. Achievement *will* come and you will learn how to figure out what to achieve and just as importantly why to achieve something.

There are certain tools and attitudes you need to be introduced to. These will help you use the program and get maximum benefits in the shortest amount of time. You have probably heard of or used these tools or attitudes at some point in your life. In order to move forward I will mention each only briefly but they will be developed further as I go through the program:

1. **Prayer:** "Pray continually."[11]   For now, just pray the best you can. If you can't do that, just talk about the good things in your life in your head.

See Action Step #3

2. **Quiet Time:**   You need to learn to be alone with yourself and more importantly, to be at peace with yourself while you are alone. The only way to get good at this is to just do it. Start small, around 5 minutes and gradually add time until you can sit quietly by yourself for at least one hour a day.

See Action Step #4

3. **Visualization:** Visualization is a tool that I have found to be extremely helpful. It is not the *key* to success, like so many programs claim, but it is a useful instrument. It comes more naturally to some people than to others. If you are already good at it, use it. If not, practice until it becomes effortless. You only need to use this for 15 minutes a day. I have found that it works best when you go to sleep 15 minutes earlier than normal and spend that time visualizing the things, behaviors and attitudes you want in your life.

See Action Step #5

4. **Have an Open Mind:** The concepts I will be discussing may seem foreign or awkward at times, but remember that you have spent most of your life learning things that work contrary to success. These are the tools and attitudes that have worked for me and countless others. Remember that you can always go back to your old ways whenever you want; just give this program an honest try first.

See Action Step #6

5. **Persistence:** Be persistent and if that doesn't seem to be working, KEEP BEING PERSISTENT! Stay with this program, it will work! You just have to keep yourself wanting a better life. Avoid comfort zones that tend to keep people down. One good way to stay with it, when it seems time to quit, is to make a list of all of the stimuli that motivates you or keeps you positive. Think of songs, poems, quotes, etc. Thomas Watson once said, "You can be discouraged by failure or you can learn from it, so go ahead and make mistakes. Make all you can. Because remember that's where you will find success."

See Action Step #7

The Beginning: Real Success

The first thing we need to determine is who you are *now*. This may seem like an easy task at first and it should be easy, but I believe that there has been so much confusion about who or what a person should be, that they might be unable to define who *they* are.   The good news is that after being involved with this program for a short time, it will become easier to answer the question: Who are you? Once you are able to answer this question clearly and truthfully, it will be easier for you to determine who you want to become.

I have found that who you are now is based on many different factors; the most important being your beliefs, experiences, decisions and personal expectations. Let's take a look at each one of these individually. We will see in a minute that they are all related.

• **Beliefs**: What you believe has an enormous impact on your actions and therefore who you are. If you believe you are successful, then you are.   If you believe you can't be successful, then you never will be.

• **Experiences:** *Every* experience - good, bad or even neutral - plays a significant role in who you have become up to this point in your life.

• **Decisions:** *Every* decision you have ever made has had a direct impact on where you are in your life today, even the small, insignificant ones.

• **Personal Expectations:** You will only go as far as you *expect* to; things can only get as good as you expect. They can also become as bad as you expect.

All of these components of who you are now, have been formed throughout your lifetime by experiences, *both* good and bad. They come from things that have happened to you. They are things that you allowed or things that were against your will. *Everything* that has happened in your life shapes who you are at this moment and as you can see from the diagram below that it is all related:

```
              Personal
             Expectations
                  ↓
  Decisions  ➡   YOU   ⬅   Beliefs
                  ↑
             Experiences
```

The chart above may at first look very complicated and intimidating, but it is actually quite simple. What I am trying to convey is the fact that who you are today has been influenced by the above components of your life. Once you understand it, it will be good news.

Let's use as an example, somebody's health, and we'll look at it from both positive and negative perspectives. Let's look at the negative first. Suppose as a child, your parents were always expecting you to catch the measles or come down with the latest strain of the flu virus. As a young, impressionable child you tended to believe your parents (personal expectations). Since you "knew" you were going to get sick, you figured why wash your hands or take any other precautions (decisions). What happened? You got sick (experiences)! Over time you began to think that it was only normal to get sick (beliefs). It was only natural that you would begin to expect yourself to continue to be sick (personal expectations, again). We could continue to go around and around this chart, as so many people do in real life, with each step strengthening the expectations, decisions, experiences and beliefs all the way through to adulthood where, today, you have a *constant* struggle to stay healthy.

You may on the other hand, have had a much more positive experience. You may have had parents who taught you that you were meant to be healthy and that your body wasn't meant to get sick (personal expectations). So what did you do? You washed your hands before eating; you ate foods that strengthened your body (decisions). Because of this, you usually were healthy and you began to see the results of your actions (experiences). So you began to expect yourself to stay healthy (beliefs). This in turn strengthened your personal expectations. Like the negative example, we can go around and around the chart to your health today; which I expect is good.

I know this to be true from personal experience, as well as from watching other people. As an adult I rarely get sick and my two children and wife are the same. This is true despite being exposed to the same "hazards" as any other people. I can see it everywhere I go. Those who expect sickness, get sickness. It is the same with every other area of your life. Following this program will help you interrupt this pattern from all four directions. You will change your personal expectations, decisions, experiences and beliefs *simultaneously*.

See Action Step #8

Another important, but difficult, way to find out about yourself is to *simply* ask someone. I know it's hard. I know it may be embarrassing. Do it *anyway*! I am sure that there are many people who will put the program down and never look at it again because of this simple request. Those who get beyond their pride and ego will learn a great deal about themselves. You will find a list of questions to ask in the activities section.

Who should you ask? Some good choices for this activity are those who know you very well. Try to find someone who knows about most aspects of your life. Someone who knows you personally, professionally and recreationally would work best. You should try to find someone who knows about your family situation too. Don't use your spouse, unless your relationship can handle a little honesty and criticism (your second time through this program you should be able to do this, but be careful your first time through). A friend, family member, or possibly someone from your church, may work your first time. Let them take form 1-9 home and *think* about the answers before writing them down. This will give you the best results. After this is completed you will have a "snap shot" of yourself. What do you think?

See Action Step #9

Do you like who you are?

If you do, that's great, but I am sure that there are areas in your life that need changing or improving, otherwise this program wouldn't have interested you.

If you don't like the results of some of the activities up to this point, then you are in the right place. I suspect that most people, who have been honest with themselves up to this point, will fall into the latter.

See Action Step #10

Remember, if you fall into the second category, stick with this program, things *will* improve. Through the course of the program you will learn to change one or more of the aspects of who you are now (beliefs, experiences, decisions and personal expectations). This will in turn cause even *more* positive changes in your life. It is called interrupting your pattern and you will learn to do it just by following through on your activities. For now, let me give you a quick way to interrupt the negative patterns in your life so that you can begin right away. It starts by visualizing the behavior that you don't like or that you want to change. While you have that visualization going on in your mind, create a second scene with the behavior you *do* want. Make the good behavior or scenario come down from the sky, crashing onto and crushing the old undesirable behavior. It sounds complicated, because experts have made it so, but just practice and you you'll get it!

See Action Step #11

Who Do You Want To Be?

It's a great question, but so few people have actually thought much about the answer. It's easy to avoid this topic, especially if you have been caught up in the world's version of success. You have probably been too busy to think this through logically but you can now. Answer this question in **Activity 12** now. Don't just write: I want to be a good person or a better spouse or a better parent. Describe your life in *detail*. Look at every facet of your life. Write about your relationships, finances, health, spirituality and any other area of your life that you would like to change or improve. Why are you doing this? Because you *become* what you think about. The Roman emperor, Marcus Aurelius said, "A man's life is what his thought makes of it."

A person who is constantly thinking about living successfully and has a clear vision of who they want to be and what they want to do will become that vision, because that is what they are focusing on. These people will have peace, serenity, happiness, success and love in their lives. A person who is constantly thinking about living in failure and does not have a clear vision will fail to live successfully. These people will live with constant fear, worry, turmoil, anger and confusion. If you spend your time thinking about nothing, you will become nothing.

See Action Step #12

Conclusion

Going back in human history, something was lost along the way. We, as humans, are no longer living the way we were intended to. We were not supposed to bury ourselves in busyness, hoping that if we just had more money, everything would be great. No, we were *meant* for a life of fulfillment. We each have a purpose and a plan that was created *especially* for us. It is our job to figure out what that purpose and plan is. That is what will fit into our lives; it will give us all of the success we want and need.

As you complete the activities for this first principle you may feel awkward and maybe even a little uncomfortable; that's okay. You are just beginning to awaken the *real* you. The you that has been buried under layers of programming you have been receiving your entire life. That feeling will fade as you get used to living your new life. It will soon be replaced by a feeling of peace, serenity and happiness that you never realized you could experience.

As you change and begin to experience real success, you may encounter resistance. In some cases this resistance may come from the people *closest* to you. Just remember these words, "if you change something and no one gets upset then you just changed something that doesn't matter."[12] You are changing something very important...YOU! The changes are for the better but people you know will get uncomfortable. Just keep moving forward and maybe one day you will be able to help them make the changes they need to make.

Principle of Success Summary

- You are created for a purpose.
- Learn to destroy your profit motive.
- To experience real success, experience failure on a massive scale.
- What success isn't: power, prestige, fame, money and material things (no one of these by themselves brings true success).
- What success is: taking the next right action.
- Achievement does not measure all success.
- Measure success by the fruit you are producing in your life.
- 7 areas of success:
  - Vision
  - Financial/Material
  - Family
  - Relationship
  - Recreational
  - Physical/Health
  - Spiritual
- Setbacks and losses are not failures
- Permanent failure is giving up or not even trying
- Real failure is sin!
- Things to remember while pursuing real success:
  - Experts complicate things.
  - Success and achievement are two different things.
  - 5 Tools and attitudes for success
  - Prayer
  - Quiet Time
  - Visualization
  - Open Mind
  - Persistence
- Determine who you are now by looking at:
  - Beliefs
  - Experiences
  - Decisions
  - Personal Expectations.
- Who do you want to be?

<u>Prayer for Success</u>

Lord Teach me about true and lasting success. Help me to see success in the things I do and in who I am on a daily basis.

Amen.

Action Steps for Success

What they are: They are small steps that you take everyday; to bring you closer to the person you want to be. They are designed to create momentum in following the FCC plan.

Why they are: People are more likely to follow through on taking action, if they don't have to figure out what actions are necessary in order to grow.

Success Action Step1 – Be Proactive

In this Action step you are going to learn how to be proactive about your success. Do something today, proactively, doing it out of pleasure and because you want to before the pain associated with it becomes too great and you are forced to act.

1. What area of your live do you need to work on today?

_____

_____

_____

2. Why have you been procrastinating doing it?

_____

_____

_____

3. What is the one proactive action you will take today toward making the change?

_____

_____

_____

4. Log your success. What are your thoughts, ideas and feelings about being proactive?

_____

_____

_____

Success Action Step 2 – Your Life

For this Action Step, I want you to imagine, briefly, that your time was up on this earth and you were given only 1 week to live. How would you answer the following questions?

1. As you reflect on your life, what do you wish you had done more of?

_____

_____

_____

2. What do you wish you had done less of?

_____

_____

_____

3. What does your life represent?

_____

_____

_____

4. What song would you want played at your funeral? Why?

_____

_____

_____

5. If you knew you had 1 week left, what would you do?

_____

_____

_____

Success Action Step 3 ~ Prayer

In this Action Step you are going to begin using prayer to help you produce success in your life. Begin by just praying about success.

1.   Set up a specific time each day when you can pray without getting interrupted. When is it? Put it on your calendar if you need to.

_____

_____

_____

2.   What areas of your life do you need to pray about?

_____

_____

_____

3.   Log your success. After spending time in prayer...how do you feel?

_____

_____

_____

_____

_____

_____

_____

_____

Success Action Step 4 – Quiet Time

For this Action Step, you are going to learn to develop a time where you can be by yourself. Do the following activities. Start by taking 5 minutes of quiet time; gradually increase it by 1 minute per day until you get to 60 minutes.

1. Set up a specific time each day when you can take quiet time without getting interrupted. When is it? Put it on your calendar if you need to.

_____

_____

_____

2. Find a place where you can take quiet time without getting interrupted. Where is it?

_____

_____

_____

3. Log your success. Use this form to write down your thoughts, ideas and feeling from your quiet time.

_____

_____

_____

_____

_____

_____

_____

_____

Success Action Step 5 – Visualize

In this Action Step you are going to practice visualizing the success you want. Go to bed 15 minutes earlier than you normally would. Spend this time visualizing the things, behaviors and attitudes you want in your life.

1. Before heading to bed get clear about what you'll be visualizing. Write down the areas that you want to focus on today. Having a clear direction for visualization will make the impact even greater.

_____

_____

_____

_____

_____

_____

2. **Log your success.** Use this form to write down your thoughts, ideas and feelings from your visualization.

_____

_____

_____

_____

_____

Success Action Step 6 – Open Mind

In this Action Step you will learn to open your mind. This will help you to overcome false beliefs that you have learned over the years that work contrary to success. With an open mind, pick one aspect of The principle of Real Success that you disagree with or don't want to do and try it.

1. What is the thing(s) mentioned in this principle that you disagree with?

_____

_____

_____

2. What are a few things that you could do to test this for its validity?

_____

_____

_____

3. Now pick one of the items listed above in number 2, and do it. Write down your thoughts, ideas and feelings after trying it out.

_____

_____

_____

4. Have your beliefs changed? Why or why not?

_____

_____

_____

Success Action Step 7 – Persistence

In this Action Step you are going to develop a set of tools to help you remain persistent, even when you are experiencing difficulties.

1.   Make a list of everything that motivates you.   Include songs, quotes, poems, etc.   Refer to this list often when you are feeling a lack of motivation.

List of motivations:

_____   _____

_____   _____

_____   _____

_____   _____

_____   _____

2.   Think of a time when you followed through during a difficult time.   What was it?

_____

_____

_____

3.   How did you get yourself to follow through?

_____

_____

_____

4.   Log your success.   What are your thoughts, ideas and feelings about persistence?

_____

_____

_____

Success Action Step 8 – Examine Your Life

In this Action Step you are going to examine your personal expectations, decisions, experience and beliefs that have influenced your life both positively and negatively.

1. Pick one area of your life that you are experiencing success in. List your personal expectations, decisions that you have made and your experiences with this area and your beliefs about this area of your life.

 a. The area of my life that is going as I want it to is:

  _____

  _____

 b. My expectations for this area are:

  _____

  _____

 c. My decision for this area have been:

  _____

  _____

 d. My experiences in this area have been:

  _____

  _____

 e. My beliefs about this area are/have been:

  _____

  _____

2. Now do the same for 1 area that isn't going so well.

 a. The area of my life that is not going as I want it to is:

  _____

  _____

 b. My expectations for this area are (what should they be?):

  _____

  _____

c. My decision for this area have been (what should they be?):

_____

_____

d. My experiences in this area have been (what should they be?):

_____

_____

e. My beliefs about this area are/have been (what should they be?):

_____

_____

Success Action Step 9 – Ask Someone

In this Action Step you are going to ask someone about yourself. Ask them the following questions and be prepared if the answers are not what you wanted or expected. Promise the person that they can be honest and you won't get mad or upset...and keep your promise!

This works best if you give them form 9-1 to fill out (on the next page). Let them think about the answers and write them down. Don't put them on the spot!

Form 9-1

Dear _____,

I am in the process of trying to improve my life with the help of Family Coaching Central (www.lifetimefundamentals.com). Part of the process is for me to pick someone I know well to tell me about myself. I picked you. Will you take a few minutes to answer these questions? I promise that I will not get angry or upset with your answers.

1. Do you know what some of the guiding beliefs in my life are?

_____

_____

_____

2. Can you tell me which experiences in my life have impacted me the most?

_____

_____

_____

3. Which of my decisions have had the most impact on my life and why?

_____

_____

_____

4. Describe my personal expectations. Am I hard/easy on myself or do I treat myself fairly?

_____

_____

_____

_____

5. What else should I know about myself from your perspective and experiences?

_____

_____

_____

_____

_____

_____

_____

_____

_____

_____

_____

_____

_____

_____

_____

_____

_____

_____

_____

_____

_____

_____

Success Action Step 10 – Do you like you?

In this Action Step you are going to be honest with yourself about *YOU*. Do the following activities:

1. Are you happy with you? If Yes, Why?

    _____

    _____

    _____

2. What can be changed to make you even better?

    _____

    _____

    _____

3. If no, what are you unhappy about?

    _____

    _____

    _____

4. Why are you unhappy about this area of your life?

    _____

    _____

    _____

5. What can be changed to make you improve?

    _____

    _____

    _____

6. What are your thoughts, ideas and feelings about yourself?

    _____

    _____

    _____

    _____

    _____

Success Action Step 11 – Interrupting Patterns

In this Action Step you are going to practice interrupting a negative pattern in order to create a new, positive behavior. Interrupt a Pattern. Practice this as often as possible. Do it until you get good at it.

1. What's the pattern/habit you want to end?

   _____
   _____
   _____

2. Why do you want to interrupt this pattern/habit?

   _____
   _____
   _____

3. What action will you take to interrupt the pattern/habit?

   _____
   _____
   _____

4. Interrupt the pattern of your behavior, as outlined on page 40. What are you thought, ideas and feelings?

   _____
   _____
   _____

5. **Log your success:** Every time you know you would have repeated this pattern/habit but didn't fall into the trap, write it down. Seeing your successes makes it easier to continue and you can also see HOW you were able to stop yourself from repeating the pattern.

_____

_____

_____

_____

_____

_____

_____

_____

_____

_____

_____

_____

_____

_____

_____

_____

_____

_____

_____

_____

_____

_____

Success Action Step 12 – Who do you want to be?

In this Action Step you are going to decide exactly what you want from life. You are going to define *your* success. Do these activities:

1. Who do you want to be?

   _____

   _____

   _____

2. Who do you want to be to your family/friends?

   _____

   _____

   _____

3. Who do you want to be professionally?

   _____

   _____

   _____

4. Who do you want to be to yourself?

   _____

   _____

   _____

5. Who do you want to be to God?

   _____

   _____

   _____

6. What do you to achieve financially?

_____

_____

_____

7. What do you want to achieve for your health?

_____

_____

_____

—

8. What are your thoughts, ideas and feelings about who you want to be?

_____

_____

_____

_____

_____

_____

_____

_____

_____

_____

_____

_____

_____

_____

_____

_____

_____

The Principle
of
Communication

Communication works for those who work
at it. – John Powell

The tongue has the power of life and death, and those
who love it will eat it's fruit.~ Proverbs 18:21 (NIV)

Communication Basics

There are many different types of people and therefore many different personalities. There are people who are social and people who are not. One thing that *everyone* has in common is our need to communicate. The ability to communicate effectively is necessary for almost every endeavor in life. We, as a society, have lost that vital skill and it's about time we learned how to get it back.

When I refer to communication, I am not referring to today's constant barrage of telemarketing calls, emails, text messages, instant messages, advertisements or anything like that. I am talking about *real* communication. The kind of communication, where what you say or do, don't say or don't do, affects you or those around you.

We will discuss communication with others, communication with God (covered in more detail in its own principle) and communication with yourself. So whether you are a completely extroverted party animal with millions of friends or a quiet introverted person who enjoys solitude, you will become better at this very *important* skill.

Some of the types of communication discussed *may* not apply to you directly, but they may in the future. It may also be nice to know the information in order to help someone else. For instance, when we discuss relationships with your children, you may not have children and have no plans to have any. It may still interest you to familiarize yourself with this section, in the event that you may have the opportunity to help a friend who has children. Regardless, I suggest you go through all of the material in this principle, even if you don't think it applies directly to you; some things may be mentioned in this Principle that aren't mentioned anywhere else in the other Principles and you may find that this particular insight helps you in your other relationships.

There are some suggestions I want to discuss before delving into the Principle Of Communication and the various people you may come into contact with on a regular basis. I have these general suggestions for communication which apply to communication with *all* people. Once I have laid a foundation, we will look at specific situations such as communication between spouses and other members of your family.

Some Suggestions About Communication

One of the biggest problems I have seen that has an impact on people's communication skills and the experiences that they have with others is their ability to criticize much, while keeping praises and complements to a minimum. In my experience, what has strengthened many of my relationships is my ability to give out more compliments than criticisms. I try to find genuine reasons to give a compliment. Most people will know if you are making things up. It is usually much easier to find what is wrong with a person and how they do things differently from you, than it is to see the positives and similarities.

See Action Step #1

Our first activity in this principle is aimed at correcting that problem. You will begin to condition yourself to start giving everyone that you need to criticize five compliments for every criticism. You may be criticizing someone because you genuinely care about the person and as the saying goes, "faithful are the wounds of a friend..."[13] You may really be trying to help, but you and the person you are communicating with will be much better served if you follow up that much needed criticism with some compliments. Also, keep in mind that you don't have to criticize someone before you give them a compliment. In fact, you should compliment people often. Learn to compliment people as a normal part of your day. I'm not saying to be fake, but rather find *real* reasons to give someone a genuine compliment. This will teach you to find the good in *everyone*, because there is good in everyone, even if you don't always think that there is.

The next suggestion I have is to learn to set clear boundaries with people. All too often in our relationships, or even in society, we generally fail to set boundaries and because of this we develop resentments. This can cause us to treat others badly; not just the one who is asking us to do more than we want or can, but *everyone* in general. You are not a super hero, nor should you want to be; don't try to do everything that is asked of you just to please other people. A good rule to live by, when asked to do something more than you want to or are willing to do, is to ask yourself how it will affect you or your family. For instance, if you are constantly being asked to work overtime at your job and the time you spend with your kids is suffering, you need to start saying no to the extra work load! It will get easier as you get used to it. I am not talking about the times when others really need your help; such as if your friend is moving and he asks you to join his moving crew as a favor or about emergencies that require your attention. It's more about the demands that are recurring that don't *fit* into your lifestyle. This will become easier and you will become better at determining what to say no to as you continue to practice this program. You will also be able to tell when someone genuinely needs your help too.

Would You Rather Be Right Or Happy?

Stop spending so much of your time and energy trying to convince others about what *you* believe or your point of view. It is a waste of time, energy and rarely accomplishes much except to get the other person mad. The best example of this is to turn on an evening talk show on one of the news networks. There you will see the greatest example of a Dale Carnegie quote: "Those convinced against their will are of the same opinion still."[14]

Many of us have never learned the true concept of communication. We are constantly trying to convince and persuade others to adopt our beliefs or point of view. We argue, many times, simply to *win* an argument. Usually we even forget what we are arguing about, but we know we must win. This type of behavior causes stress and takes energy we could be using on many different activities.

We live in a world of differing viewpoints. That will never change. What can change is *our* attitude and response to other people. We can help other people much more, by simply *listening* to them, than by trying to convince them of something. Even if we know we are right, by simply letting someone get their own point of view across, they begin to realize their own flawed thinking. There are many times when just letting someone else speak is extremely worthwhile.

If we try to argue with them, they begin to see us as a threat and become determined to win an argument rather than have a discussion. They begin to see the conversation as a battle that must be won, rather than a chance to look at their own beliefs. It is *our* responsibility to listen to others. Many people in the world are lost. They need someone to listen to them, so that they can begin to find their way.

Stop trying to win arguments! Very rarely will that help people understand and accept the truth. Many times, it will push people away from the truth *permanently*.

Instead of trying to "win" arguments, accept and acknowledge that everyone has a *different* point of view and that being born with freedom, we are entitled to that point of view. An argument or disagreement can usually be diffused by acknowledging the other point of view, even if the other person is wrong and/or you completely disagree. It is true that, "where we stand depends on where we sit,"[15] meaning that our particular opinion or view of a situation or set of circumstances is *directly* related to the frame of mind we are viewing it from. We almost always view the world and what is happening in it according to our own life experiences. The next time somebody says something that makes you angry or upset (you probably won't have to wait long), remember that their unique experiences may have brought them to this point. Just listen and don't try to persuade them to accept your point of view. Not only will you learn to develop patience, but you will also have a much better chance of them eventually looking at you and your life as an example.

Rather than wasting your *valuable* time, energy and resources trying to convince others about something, I have found that, if you are living correctly, it is much better and easier to set your own life as an example for people to watch and follow.

Ten Rules For Communication

I have developed these ten rules for communication, which when implemented, have far more power than any argument could ever have.

1. **Speak The Truth In Love:** This does not mean that you can say *anything* you want. It is not being rude or ill mannered. However, it is saying what needs to be said, but in a spirit of true compassion, making sure that you are motivated by love. I may be sitting down with a friend and saying, "Hey Mary, I have noticed you've been drinking a lot lately, is everything okay?" Instead of, "Hey Mary, you're so disgusting. You are such a loser drinking so much."

2. **Speak Life:** Your tongue has a great deal of power. By what you say, you can set someone's dream in motion or you can stop it dead in its tracks. Don't be the person who always squashes somebody's hopes. Instead, be someone who encourages others to find their life vision. Encourage

somebody who needs to hear nice words. If you don't have nice words, then don't say anything. Speaking life may take the form of just plain encouragement or it may be redirecting someone to find their true calling.

3. **Speak Empowerment:** Help someone else *believe* in who they are and what they can do. Sometimes the person you are communicating with just needs to know that you believe in what they can do. The best example of this is when Danielle signed me up for karate. She knew that I had wanted to take lessons since I was a child and I got in to the habit of delaying this. The day she came home and told me that she had signed me up for classes, I knew she believed in me and that in turn gave me the confidence I needed to start my lessons.

4. **Speak Positively:** We all know that person. The one who can take *any* situation and find the negative. Don't be that person! Is your presence in a group or with another individual negative, neutral or positive? You can figure this out by stopping to pause during your communications with other people. Figure out if people become more negative or positive when you get involved, or if they just stay the same. What do you bring to the table?

5. **Speak Forgiveness:** "Be kind and compassionate to one another, forgiving each other..."[16] Learn to accept an apology; the only one who is being hurt when you don't, is *you*. By accepting the apology, you are not forgetting what happened, you are simply acknowledging the other party involved and in the process, relieving yourself from the stress and pain of holding on to something hurtful from the past. Also, make sure you are seeking forgiveness for your mistakes. (This is discussed in more detail in another principle). *Always* be quick to admit when you are wrong.

6. **Speak Praise:** *Always* try to catch somebody doing something right. It's easy to point out when somebody makes a mistake, but make sure you are also telling them when they do a good job. Do this for everyone you come in contact with, whether it is the clerk at the grocery store or the waitress at your favorite restaurant. You never can tell whose life you are influencing. Remember that, "to the world you might be one person, but to one person you might be the world."[17] Strive to always build others up.

7. **Be Kinder Than Necessary:** There is a phrase that goes, "Say what you mean. Mean what you say but don't say it

mean." Remember to be nice to *everyone*; even people that you may not necessarily like. Always go out of your way to be kind to the people you come in contact with. "You have heard it said, 'Love your neighbor and hate your enemy.' But I tell you: love your enemies and pray for those who persecute you'"[18]

8. **Never Say But:** When you use this word, you are conveying to the other person that there are conditions that must be met before you do your part. Some examples would be: "I want to spend time with you *but* I have to work late." or "I forgive you *but*...(fill in the blank). Most people have discovered that by using this one simple word you can also avoid any responsibility; such as, "Yes, I was late for work, *but* my alarm didn't go off." Anything after "but" is just an excuse or rationalization; so avoid the buts.

9. **Take Off The Mask:** The easiest way to say this is to say, "*just be yourself.*" So many people today have created this false persona or personality. Many people choose to do this because of the safety and predictability found in being someone we *think* others will like. The people who are just themselves tend to shine through. It's very unlikely that you are really fooling anyone with your "tough guy" image or your false wisdom; so just try being yourself. "Therefore each of you must put off falsehood and speak truthfully to his neighbor, for we are all members of one body. 'In your anger do not sin': Do not let the sun go down while you are still angry..."[19]

10. **Listen:** The Greek philosopher, Epictetus, said it best: "We have two ears and one mouth so that we can listen twice as much as we speak." If we would only LISTEN to that advice, we would be able to learn so much. Listening is the best communication tool of all because when we listen, we convey the message that we truly care. When we just talk, waiting to respond, rather than listening and responding after hearing the other person, we fail to communicate effectively.

If you are living a good life and sticking to all the Principles of this program, then the example of your life will be the *best* proof of all. By your actions and the results you get in your life, on a consistent basis, you will be able to convince people without saying a word that you have found a better way of life and have uncovered the truth.

See Action Step #2

Three Questions To Ask Yourself Before You Say Anything

Many times it's easy to say something that shouldn't be said. Sometimes, because of anger, excitement or any other emotion, we say things that are better left unsaid. It has happened to us all, but it's more than just a slip of the tongue. It is an ingrained behavior that needs to be addressed and corrected so that we can help to bring success and happiness to others, as well as ourselves. Obviously, as we previously discussed, there are many times that we need to speak up, but there are also many times when it may be better to keep our comments to ourselves. "Do you see a man who speaks in haste? There is more hope for a fool than for him."[20] Many times it is a hard decision, but with the tools you are developing in this program, it will become much easier.

Here are the questions you should ask yourself *before* speaking:

- **Does it need to be *said*?** The classic example is if someone leaves the cap off the toothpaste. Is it really that important that you would be willing to get into an argument about it?

- **Does it need to be *said now*?** Maybe it is something that needs to be said, but does it have to be said in this instant? If you have a friend who just got into a fender bender at the grocery store, is now the time to criticize their driving skills? It would probably be better to let some time pass and allow their tension to ease.

- **Does it need to be said now by *you*?** You might be in the movie theater one day and see an out of control child. Yes, the parents should learn to control their child, but they are in line to see a different movie than you. Let it go. It isn't your situation to get involved in.

  See Action Step #3

Communication and Learning Styles

Let's thank God for making us all very different and unique. We all develop different personalities and ways to interact with the world around us. Could you imagine how boring our world would be if we *all* responded to the same stimuli in exactly the same way? There would be no variety or spice to life. However, having all these differences does make our relationships and our attempts at learning a bit more complicated. Once explained, people's communication and learning styles do become much easier to understand, especially with practice. Before I begin discussing these communication and learning styles, keep in mind that no two people are alike and most people have a blend of *more* than one style. Some people may even have a communication style that is different from their learning style. The three styles that I will discuss in this program are visual, auditory and feeling oriented (the "experts" refer to this as kinesthetic) people.

Visual people tend to want to use their sense of sight. They may say things like: "Can't you *see* that I love you?" or "I *see* how you solved that math problem." They like to use words and actions that suggest sight or other visual stimulus. Some other words or actions that visual people may use, include (but aren't limited to): look, see, show, etc. They will need to see a task done before they can do it themselves and if they are trying to explain something, they will want to show you or write down instructions.

These people need to see body language and facial expressions to fully grasp what is going on. They probably think in pictures and appreciate visual displays such as diagrams, signs, written instructions or notes.

Auditory people tend to want to use their sense of hearing. They may say things like: "Did you *hear* what I said?" or "The answer to that problem *sounds* good." They like to use words that suggest sound or other auditory stimuli. Some other words or actions that auditory people use may include (but aren't limited to): tell, listen, told, etc. They will need you to explain the instructions to them before they begin. If they are trying to explain something, they will be very detailed in their directions.

These people enjoy discussions, listening to what other people have to say and talking things out. They listen and make judgments based on tone of voice, speed and pitch; written information means very little until it is heard.

Feeling oriented people tend to use their sense of touch and feelings. They like to move and absorb information. They communicate by doing and touching. They may say things like: "I don't feel like you understand me," or "The answer to that problem feels right." They will need to perform a task rather than watching someone else or listening to instructions in order to understand it.

Feeling oriented people tend to rely on feelings and touch. Some other words they use may include: feel, touch, experience, etc. They may think it's important to shake hands or they may be the one who gives out a lot of hugs during the holidays.

These people enjoy a hands-on approach to relationships. They actively explore the world around them. It may be hard for them to sit still for long periods of time and they may become distracted without the ability to explore.

These are the 3 basic communication and learning styles that you encounter. Remember that most people are a combination of more than one style and probably will not fit neatly into those described above. As with anything, these can be made much more complicated, if you want. I prefer to stick to the basics and the "KEEP IT SIMPLE" method; it works better. Learn to recognize these traits in others and when it comes time to communicate with them, or teach them something, using your new knowledge in this area, you will be able to make the experience as smooth and comfortable as possible for everyone involved. As with anything, the more you *practice* recognizing and adapting to other people's styles the better you will get.

See Action Step #4

Communication With Your Family

The importance of communication is frequently talked about with regards to successful relationships, sadly however, failure to communicate is *very* common in families today. The problem lies in the fact that there is so much pressure placed on families by society. We are told how we should act and what we should do. Everybody is trying to stuff so much into their lives that communication gets put on the back burner. As one fails to communicate, the tension builds and it becomes a downward spiral, until the unfortunate point is reached where the family begins to deteriorate. You can see it in families all around you. Unfortunately, many families have turned into "war zones."

There is a better way! In fact, if you haven't realized it, you should have peace and happiness in *your* family. Your family should enrich your life, not make you stressed out. We, as a society, have gotten away from this *simple* fact. We should all spend time praying for a society that gets *back* to the point where we, once again, honor and respect the family structure. Hopefully, that will happen one day. The good news is that YOU don't have to wait on society. You can begin, right now, improving your family life and making it something that *everyone* can enjoy.

We need to be clear about what communication is and what it is not. Communication *is* expressing your needs, expectations, emotions, etc. clearly and directly. Don't expect your spouse, children or other family members to be able to read your mind or your body language.

So how do you build a successful family? My experience has been to do *all* of the following things and to do them *all* of the time. Obviously, there will be times when you make mistakes, but keep trying to improve. Remember, when it comes to your current family, there are no do-overs. In twenty years, you won't be able to go back and decide that you want to build your family up and make it strong. Do these things *today*! What you do today will have a direct impact on your family today and for generations to come.

Spend Time Together. Spend as much time as possible with your family. It shouldn't hurt or be stressful. It should be enjoyable, fun and fulfilling. You should want and seek to spend as much time as possible with them. I know that for the majority of people I meet, my family seems like aliens because we spend so much time together. I know that we make people "sick" with our hellos and good-byes, when we do have to part company for school, business meetings, exercise, etc. We don't care! This is what God had intended for families. Remember, that up until the early part of the 20th Century, families were together most of the day. They were working on the farm or doing other chores. It wasn't until the industrialization and commercialism of the last century began, that so many families started to weaken and fall apart. The good news is that yours doesn't have to.

Many people don't even realize what they are doing; it has just become automatic. My family and I had attended a function at our son's school, put on by the school's Father's Club. It was a movie night, where they were playing a kid's movie, meant to be enjoyed by the entire family. I had to chuckle a little bit, as we walked by the gymnasium and saw a large number of the fathers playing basketball with each other, instead of sitting with their families watching the movie.

Eat Together. One of the *easiest* ways to spend time together is to eat together. Spend at least one meal per day (I prefer two or three) together. Talk about everyone's day and after the meal is over, clean up together. After the cleaning is done; sit down and read together. You get the point; spend time *together*.

I've heard so many excuses for not doing this simple thing, such as: "We are just to busy to eat together," or "We have different schedules." This is complete nonsense. You can make it work if you're committed.

Forget the excuses and *find* the time. Here are some suggestions that may help:

- **Monthly/Weekly cooking:** Do all of your cooking one day a week or month and freeze the meals until you are ready to use them.

- **Find healthy prepared dinners:** Buy a week or month's worth of prepared dinners from a restaurant or caterer and freeze them until you are ready to eat.

- **Create a "dinner exchange":** Find several other families with similar likes and have each one cook several days worth of meals for *all* of the families. Meet once a week or month to exchange the meals. Freeze until needed.

Now there are no excuses for not eating together. If you *really* want to, you will find a way!

See Action Step #5

Practice Acceptance. Another way to strengthen your family is to make sure there is acceptance in your relationships. This acceptance needs to be *complete*. In no way should acceptance be conditional or based on anything, other than the fact that the other person is your husband, wife, son or daughter. It should not matter what anyone's likes or dislikes are. Remember that you are working together, as a team, to build strong bonds that will *overcome* the negative pull of popular culture and society. There are many ways to do this, but what works for my family is finding out as much information as possible about each other. Do you know your son's favorite food? Do you know your daughter's favorite color? Do you know your wife's favorite TV show? Do you know your husband's favorite activity? Well, you should! If you don't know, then take the time to find out what those things are.

I like to do two things that, I think, help to *improve* acceptance within my family. The first one is to find out what everyone's favorite activity is...and do it! Do it at least once a week. The next thing is to find an activity you *all* enjoy; something that you all have in common and do it. My family has several; we all enjoy martial arts and hiking. We do these activities together, many times during the week. They keep us all in good shape and they create many great memories. We also enjoy eating popcorn, ice cream and watching a good movie.

The point is that the acceptance in your family should not be based on how smart, beautiful or talented someone is. It should be based simply on who they are in relation to you.

See Action Step #6

Respect Each Other. Respect is very important in families. Without respect, people tend to put their own needs and wants before others. There is no sacrifice for others and self-ambition begins to blind everyone involved. Many times, this leads to unchecked resentment and cynicism. A family that values respect is a *happy* family. Kids should know that, without a doubt, they are important. Spouses should know that even though they don't always agree on *every* topic, there is still love, respect and acceptance. There should be respect for each other's beliefs, thoughts and property. In my home, for example, we don't always agree on the best way to discipline our children, but we *do* agree to discuss each others point of view and from there, decide on the best course of action. We know that we both have differing experiences, but there is *respect* for those differences. Our children don't always play as nicely together as we would like but they both know that it is important to treat each other's toys appropriately. This respect for each other is so important to allowing us to grow closer together that we value it and constantly work on it.

Be A Place Of Safety And Security. A family should be a place of safety and security. Let's face it, the world is a *tough* place. We spend a great deal of time out in the world. When we get home, we should come to a place where we can let our guard down and relax. As we head for home, after a long day, we should begin to feel more relaxed as we get closer, not more stressed out. I remember talking to a guy who told me, that as he got close to home after a long day at work, he would find a parking lot to sit in, so that he could relax and get ready for the turmoil he was about to enter as he got home. In other words, he dreaded going home. This is a horrible place to be. If that is your experience, then it *needs* to change. You need to experience feelings of safety and security as you approach.

You also need to *provide* safety and security to those you love. They need to know that they can depend on you and that you will *protect* them, no matter what the circumstances. You will stick up for them and stick by them, even if they are wrong! Yes, they should learn right from wrong, but when a crisis arises and they *need* you, it is not the time to be teaching lessons. There will be turbulence and trials in this world. Will you be there for those you love the most? Will they be there for you? The answer to both of these questions should be an absolute yes, without any hesitation or doubt.

Listen To Each Other. When it comes to communication, many people, as we discussed earlier, fail to grasp the *importance* of listening. Listening is a practice that is very difficult for most. By listening completely and seeking to understand the person who is speaking, you will be showing the speaker that you *really* care about what they have to say. The fact that you are really listening to them will be evident in your body language and in your facial expressions and they will most likely give you the same courtesy when it's your turn to speak. If you are more concerned with your next comment or with *your* agenda in the conversation, it will be evident and may not give you a desired result or outcome in the conversation. *Always* seek to listen!

I have had *many* experiences with my children when I was beginning to get angry, but when they explained a particular action, it was clear that there was no reason for discipline. In these circumstances, the outcomes would be much different if I did not take the time to listen.

The same is true for my interactions with my wife. Many disagreements have been diverted or resolved, *simply* because we took the time to listen. I have also discovered that many times we are saying the same thing, but are using different words. Without taking the time to listen to each other, these situations could easily erupt into something *more* than a simple conversation.

Everyone in your home, no matter age or any other circumstances, should *always* know that their voice will be heard and that they will be able to communicate their desires, needs, beliefs and wishes. This should be done in an atmosphere of peace, without having to yell. I grew up in a family where the only verbal communication that existed was yelling at each other. If you disagreed, the way to resolve it would be to start calling the other person names or to mount some other type of verbal assault. As could be expected, there wasn't much peace in my home as a child.

Each Relationship Is Different. You should treat each relationship differently. It's obvious, that my relationship with my wife will be much *different* than my relationship with my son or daughter. Even among children, there should be different relationships. I do not do the same things with my daughter as with my son. First, my son is older so he has more life experience. He is better able to reason. Their personalities are also very different. I am learning that the way I discipline them needs to be much different. With my son, when I am getting him to clean up his toys, the *suggestion* that I will take something away if he doesn't follow through works well. This method, however, doesn't work so well with my daughter. For her, I need to sit down with her and *actually* tell her what to do. This is something that needs to be remembered, because it will have an enormous impact on the *effectiveness* of your communication.

Following these simple steps in communication, will open your family up to each other and will create an atmosphere of mutual respect for all. You will have a successful family life.

Communication With Your Husband or Wife

We have all sat through a wedding ceremony, if not participated in one of our own and this is roughly what we heard, or agreed to:

> *I, (name), take you (name), to be my (wife/husband), to have and to hold from this day forward, for better or for worse, for richer, for*

poorer, in sickness and in health, to love and to cherish; from this day forward until death do us part.

That's it! That's all you have to do to have a long, happy marriage. If you are already married, start doing what you promised to. If you are not married yet, but are in a relationship with the one you intend to marry, then start doing this stuff now, before the wedding. There's nothing wrong with getting a head start. If you're not in a relationship now and have no plans to get married, learn this anyways because the day *will* come when you will meet someone who is that special to you.

Here are some additional tips that I have found to be useful in my marriage and I believe have strengthened the relationship between my wife and myself.

I have also found it helpful to read Ephesians 5:22-33 and *highly* recommend it when you have two spare minutes. It gives very clear direction as to what each party of the marriage should do. The roles are *clearly* defined; it's when we, as a society, begin to change these roles and manipulate them that problems occur in marriages.

You must be willing to do all of the following things in your relationship and to be the first one to do them, even if your partner does not seem to be responding:

1. **Take off the mask.** It is very likely that your spouse knows who you are under all of the layers. It is why they decided to marry you in the first place. They probably miss the person that has been hidden under the mask you have decided to wear.

2. **Apologize.** Just do it, even if *you're* not wrong. It will ease tension and most likely cause the other person to admit they were wrong too. Even if it doesn't "work" the way you want it to, you will still feel better.

3. **Share your feelings.** *Tell* them how you are feeling. Let them know if you are going through a time of uncertainty or if you feel very secure. It will go a long way, most times, toward explaining your words or actions.

4. **Share your fears.** Being able to tell the one you *should* trust most what you are afraid of or what worries you will do incredible things to help you conquer these fears and worries.

5. **Praise/compliment them.** Remember the rule – give five compliments for *every* criticism. That rule applies here as well however, remember to also give complements and praise, even if there is no criticism.

6. **Be grateful.** The person you chose to spend your life with still has a lot to offer. Not everyone is as *fortunate* as you to have this person in his or her life. Thank them for who they are and thank God for bringing them into your life. Never take them for granted!

7. **Do something nice.** Do something that they like and appreciate. This is best done after figuring out their communication and learning styles. Some examples are: sing them a song (auditory), write a poem (visual) or give them a massage (feeling oriented). Do caring things *often.*

8. **Listen.** Let them talk about *themselves.* Don't say anything, except to ask questions about *them.* Let them talk about *their* interests. Let *them* talk about all of the things covered in this section.

Do these things *often* and your relationship with your husband or wife will continue to improve. This is important, since life has a tendency to overwhelm us and cause us to stray from the simple things that allow for continued growth. If you think about it, you probably did all of the things listed above when you first met and that's why you fell in love. Resume where you left off.

See Action Step #7

Two Small But Significant Points

There are several other small points to make, but they are very *significant* in nature. The first is to be aware whom you associate with as a family and as a couple. Make sure you are not spending time socially with people whose relationship is a mess. Do not associate with couples that argue, fight or disagree in public. If they do that in the open, think of how complicated their relationship must be behind closed doors. It is poison. Give them help, guidance and directions (when and if it's asked for) and be a positive example, but don't be involved socially with them.

Also, talk about children, *before* you have children. Iron out the differences or possible differences, well in advance, so that there will be no big surprises when they come. This will make life much less stressful. Here are some areas that should be discussed (of course there are many more):

- **Religion/Spirituality:** What are you going to teach them and why?

- **Diet:** Are they going to have a high fructose corn syrup based diet or will you stress fruits and vegetables?

- **Discipline:** How will you discipline them and under what circumstances?

- **Parental Responsibilities:** Whose job is it to do what?

- **Anything else you can think of!**

It's okay to have differing opinions on these topics, but decide whose methods will be used and enforced. It will make the child rearing years much more peaceful.

Communication With Your Children

This is one of the most important things you will *ever* do. It is more important than any career or job you pursue. You need to take communication with your kids *very* seriously, but also have fun! With most things in life, if you mess up you can go back and redo it; it is different with your children. If you wake up and realize, when your kids are out of high school, that you didn't do such a great job, you can't go back and fix it. That's not to say that you can't go back and make amends for mistakes of the past, but you can't redo your children's childhood.

I remember trying to explain this to a guy who belongs to a spiritual group that I participate in. He had grown children of his own. My family was in the midst of a financial storm and I had mentioned a trip that we were taking, as a family. He tried to make me feel guilty for taking a vacation, when I owed other people money. I attempted to explain to him about the limited time that we have with our children while they are young and that I would still owe the money and can pay it later. He didn't understand but I know that I made the right decision.

Understand "Generational Curses." When you began this program, you may have been suffering under what is called a "generational curse"[21]. Before I go any further, let's understand what I mean by a "generational curse." It is clear that God does not punish people for their parents sins[22]. It is also clear though, that your children will struggle with the *same* things that you struggle with, unless *you* do something about it. It's up to you to break the negative cycle of your family, past and present.

"Our parents are the victims of their parents' ignorance. Unless we learn to think differently, our children will be the victims of our ignorance."[23] In other words, if you struggle with organization, it is very likely that your children will also be disorganized, unless you take real, concrete steps to correct this problem. This has very little to do with spirituality and absolutely nothing to do with God; it is simply learned behavior. A child looks to his parents for guidance. The behaviors that he witnesses become "normal" to him. I remember growing up in a larger family that consumed a lot of alcohol. As a child and for most of my life, I believed that excessive drinking was normal behavior and that everyone did it. Obviously, I found out later that not every family exhibited this behavior, but for a long time I was blind to the truth.

So how do you break a "generational curse" and avoid passing it on to your children and instead *shower* your kids with "generational blessings?" It's really quite simple. I'm not saying it's easy, but it is simple. The first thing to do, is to recognize the re-occurring behaviors[24]. Once you have done this, you need to change those behaviors[25]. Most importantly, ask God for help and He *will* help you[26]. By doing these things, along with *everything* else you are learning in this program, you will be able to overcome the challenges of the past and begin to form a brighter future for yourself and your children.

The first thing you need to do is to *choose* "generational blessing": "this day I call heaven and earth as witnesses against you that I have set before you life and death, blessings and curses. Now choose life, so that you and your children may live."[27]

Next, realize that your words and actions of today, no matter how significant or insignificant will echo for generations to come. I am reminded of a story that I came across several years ago. The story is about 2 men. Both men lived in the 1700's. The first man, Max Jukes, was an immoral man and a moonshiner. He chose not to go to church and married a woman with similar character. The second man, Jonathan Edwards, was a God loving minister who is said to have started the Great Awakening by his teachings. He also married a woman with character similar to his own.

What's not surprising is the path their descendants took through life. Max Jukes had 1,026 descendants. Of these, 300 died prematurely, 100 were sent to prison, 190 were prostitutes and 100 were alcoholics. On the other hand, Jonathan Edwards had 729 descendants. Of these, 300 were preachers, 65 were college professors, and 13 were authors.

Do you see the connection? I hope so. What you say and do with your children *matters* more than most people will ever realize. You will begin to realize it too when you do the next Action Step.

See Action Step #8

In addition to everything covered in the "Communication With Other People" section, you should also do the following, while keeping in mind the importance of what you are doing. Remember, "train a child in the way he should go and when he is old he will not turn from it."[28]

- **Empower your kids.** Empower them to be successful, confident and competent. Make sure they know how to navigate in this crazy place, we call the world. There are many things you can do to help them. The most important of these is to lead by *example*. Your children will learn from your cues. For example, don't tell your kids about how bad "junk food" is, while you're stuffing your face with donuts. Not only will the message fail to register, but if this behavior continues, as they get older, they will begin to see you as a hypocrite.

- **Teach your kids everything you can.** Your kids are looking to *you* for guidance. Sometimes it doesn't seem like it, but they are. You have an incredible opportunity to teach them, so use the chance wisely. Remember, your children are *looking* for a role model; someone to follow and respect. You should be the one to fill that role. If you don't fill it, they will fill it for themselves. Don't let Tiger Woods or some other misguided figure from Hollywood or the sports-world fill that void. You fill the role and there *won't* be a void.

- **Teach your kids about the world.** Teach them as much as you know. If you don't know something that you need to teach them, learn it *with* them. Make sure that you teach objectively and without bias. Teach them that sometimes there *are* choices to make and sometimes there *aren't*. For example, teach them that in order to be healthy, they *must* eat their vegetables. They can *choose* however, whether to eat broccoli or spinach. Maybe you don't like vegetables; don't let that bias have an impact on *their* eating habits. Also, teach your kids about things you may think they are learning somewhere else. I routinely teach and practice with my kids things you would expect them to learn in school. I have decided not to leave math, reading, science or any other subject I think is important up to the school system. It is my responsibility. My kids are above average and doing work that exceeds their grade level. I am sure you can make the connection.

- **Encourage them to try something new.** This will help them to define their *own* direction and help them to figure out what they were created to do. Let them try new things in several different areas, such as: sports, music, hobbies and other interests. The more positive experiences they have, the more likely they are to find their life's purpose. Also, teach them about new things they *shouldn't* be trying, such as sex or drugs. Encourage them to seek your guidance, before trying something they are unsure of.

- **Teach you kids about God[29].** If you struggle in this area yourself, maybe they can teach you. Children have an innocence about them that allows them to understand a simple topic, such as God, that has been so complicated by the world. Read your Bible together. Pray together. Go to church together. Some of the best times we have together, as a family, is when we are praying, studying God's word or when we are actually *applying* His word in our lives. We run the Sunday School Program at our church and our son has helped since he was in kindergarten. As our daughter gets older she will help too. Both of our kids help with our high school ministry work. Yes, they are much younger than the high school kids but they are still able to offer so much. If you need to, find God together.

- **Teach your kids about success.** Teach them what it is. Teach them how to get it. Use this program as a guide. Allow them to learn the difference between *real* success and the world's version of success. Point out the differences between the success you enjoy in your life and the false success celebrated by others. Also, point out, whenever possible, examples of people choosing what they *think* success is. As a parent, you are the most powerful influencer of your child's current and future behavior. As I said earlier, set an example! When your children see real success in your life, they begin to understand it. When they see the "love, joy, peace, patience, kindness, goodness, faithfulness, gentleness and self-control"[30] leading to good things in your life, they will develop a *concrete* meaning of success. You will be inviting your children into a way of life that will sustain them and allow them to thrive, long after they leave home.

See Action Step #9

Stages of Development

It's important to know the stages your children will grow through and how you can be there to help them and to encourage them through each of these stages. It's also important to examine the stages you went through growing up. This will help to give you insight into who you are today. They do not happen at exactly the same time for everyone, but you will be able to get a rough idea as to when each stage begins and how long it will last. The three stages we need to discuss are the:

1. Beginning years

2. Searching years

3. Real World years.

Like most things in this program, it is not as hard as the "experts" would make you think.

The Beginning Years

These years are *experimental* in nature. The acquisition and development of life skills begins long before the ability to understand the abstract nature of these skills sets in. Your children need to feel a sense of belonging, positive experiences, a shared identity, and positive reinforcement. Make these lessons consistent and positive. Teach them, by *example*, about success and the skills necessary to succeed. Read motivational literature. Teach them a can do attitude. Listen to positive, uplifting and motivational music. Begin to develop positive habits; these habits can be anything from brushing teeth to planning out your day and sticking to a schedule. Also, develop good behaviors such as saying please and thank you. Teach them to pick up after themselves and to hold the door open for other people. Teach them to develop strong, positive friendships. Teach them that life is not something to face alone. Life should be an experience that should be shared with people who support them, pray for them and who they support and pray for in return.

The Searching Years

This stage usually begins in the teenage years. Your children begin to develop an *exploratory* attitude (if you have planted the proper seeds, there is no need to worry). They begin to question the things that they have been taught and try to develop a sense of independence. They may go through a period of deep personal struggle regarding the direction of their lives. This period can last anywhere from a couple of months to several years, or more. It is a *critical* time, when many young people become caught up in worldly "success."

In this stage, many people lose their sense of belonging and seek other groups to fit into. They have not lost the lessons they have been taught; they are just not sure if those lessons are compatible with who they are. Your children need the following:

- They need a secure environment where they can *challenge* what they have learned, and express alternate views.

- They need to be exposed to experiences that will spur their emotional and intellectual thinking.

- They need to develop adult mentors, outside of their families, to validate the lessons that they have been taught. (teachers, youth leaders, etc.)

- They need positive experiences

- They also need to experience hurt and defeat.

- They need to know that *you* trust them and will be there to support them, if they need it.

The Real World

The "Real World" is where most people will spend the greatest amount of time so it is very important that the lessons learned in the other two stages of development have relevance for what will be encountered in this stage.

As you were reading the other two stages of development, if you thought to yourself, "wow I have been doing all of these things perfectly throughout my children's entire lives and I was taught these lessons very thoroughly when I was young," then you will have no worries when your kid's enter this stage. However, if you are like most of us, read on.

The "Real World" is a scary place at first. The things you do in this stage have lasting consequences. Even if someone entering this stage doesn't realize it at first, they quickly learn that fact.

So, what can you do for someone entering this important stage in their life? There are several things I think are important to help someone in this stage of life:

- **Let them make their *own* mistakes.** It is important to make mistakes. In fact, for most people, many valuable lessons are learned by failure and mistakes.

- **Let them know that mistakes aren't permanent.** I believe that there are no failures or mistakes that can not be corrected and you must pass that wisdom on to your children.

- **Let them enjoy their own success; it's theirs, not yours.** Even though you may have taught them many valuable lessons throughout their life, do not take credit for their success.

- **Let them know that successes aren't permanent.** Just because they were successful last week or even yesterday, they must continue to work on future success.

- **Be there for them.** Your kids will need your help and guidance far into adulthood. Be there for them. Help them when possible but do not help them in areas you know nothing about. If they need help and you can't offer assistance, guide them in finding someone who can.

- **Only help when asked.** Do not help your kids in this stage unless *they* ask. If you know that they need assistance but aren't asking you, it may be that there are lessons they must learn on their own before approaching you. Be patient.

Discipline Your Kids

It seems that discipline has become such a forbidden topic in society. People are afraid to talk about it, think about it or do it! The only problem with this line of thinking is that we are hurting the very ones we are *trying* to protect. We, as a society, have become so afraid of hurting our children's pride and ego, that we give them no direction. They are lost! Our quest to raise self-confident children has caused us to miss the mark on competence. I see it everywhere, from the toddler throwing a tantrum in the candy isle at the grocery store, to the teenager who kills a carload of his friends in an accident. It is your *responsibility* and your *duty* to discipline your children. Take it seriously and they will be far ahead of the crowd as they enter this stage we just discussed, "The Real World." Fail to do it and they will be lost. One of my biggest regrets, from my childhood, is my parent's lack of discipline. Yes, I did get in trouble and sometimes I even got *"punished"* for my bad behavior. The only problem is, they never followed through with those *punishments* and I suffered for it.

I am not talking about severe punishment or being hard on your kids here. I am talking about a planned attempt and follow through at giving your children guidance and direction. I am talking about teaching them the proper way to act. They need to be taught about obligations and responsibilities. They need to be taught the importance of following through on commitments. In fact, "wise discipline imparts wisdom; spoiled adolescents embarrass their parents. Discipline your children; you will be glad you did- they'll turn out delightful to live with."[31] When they get older, they will be grateful too!

Communication with Yourself

This is a very important aspect of communication that most people rarely think of, or tend to miss altogether, but you *need* to take care of you! When you take care of you, it becomes much *easier* to take care of and help the other people around you. You begin to value yourself and therefore begin to value those around you more. If you have ever been on an airplane, during the pre-flight safety demonstrations, there is a reason they tell you that if the oxygen masks are deployed, that you should put yours on first. If you start by putting on your children's mask, or trying to help others around you, there's a good chance that you will get panicky or lose control.

By not taking care of yourself first, you become useless to everyone and won't be able to help anyone. On the other hand, if you put your mask on first, you will remain calm and relaxed; therefore you will be better able to serve and help those around you. This is not an invitation to be selfish and neglectful of others, using the excuse that you have to take care of yourself first; but if you are practicing the *rest* of this program, that will not be an issue, you will instinctively know what to do.

The first thing you need to do, is *examine* the lessons you learned as a child. There is a good chance that many of these lessons were passed on to you by well-meaning people. If they were negative lessons, they need to be corrected. If they were positive lessons, they need to be strengthened and reinforced. What I have discovered, is that there is a *direct* relationship between the life you are living now and the lessons you learned as a child. For example, look at the list of learned behaviors and the outcomes they lead to. I have done this for both negative and positive behaviors, below. Some of these may be hard truths to accept but they are *necessary* for your continued growth.

Negative lessons:

- If a child experiences criticism, they learn self-doubt.
- If a child experiences hostility, they learn anger.
- If a child experiences rejection, they learn shyness.
- If a child experiences resentment, they learn shame.
- If a child experiences dishonesty, they learn deceit.
- If a child experiences extreme or ongoing lack, they learn poverty.

Positive lessons:

- If a child experiences patience, they learn understanding.
- If a child experiences success, they learn confidence.
- If a child experiences praise, they learn encouragement.
- If a child experiences discipline, they learn justice.
- If a child experiences prayer, they learn faith.
- If a child experiences approval, they learn acceptance.

This list contains only a small sampling of the possible lessons you learned as a child because of what you experienced. To make a complete list would be impossible.

"If you think in negative terms, you will get negative results. If you think in positive terms, you will achieve positive results."[32] We are what our *thoughts* have made us. We are in our current situation, good or bad, because of our thoughts. Our thoughts tell our brain what we deserve, so if you are constantly dwelling on negative thoughts about yourself and the world around you that is exactly what your brain will produce in your life. You will have a future based upon your thoughts *today*. The power to change your tomorrow begins with your thinking of today. Make an effort and make it a serious effort to change your thinking and you will change your tomorrow. Your life is the sum total of what you have allowed into your mind. Guard it carefully to insure happiness, peace and serenity.

"Do not be anxious about anything, but in everything, by prayer and petition, with thanksgiving, present your requests to God. And the peace of God, which transcends all understanding, will guard your hearts and your minds in Christ Jesus. Finally, brothers, whatever is true, whatever is noble, whatever is right, whatever is pure, whatever is lovely, whatever is admirable—if anything is excellent or praiseworthy—think about such things."[33]

See Action Step #10

Be Content, Not Satisfied.   Don't confuse these two conditions.   There is a difference.   Contentment is being at peace with where you are *now*.   It is being able to live with yourself at your present stage of life.   It is not wanting to settle down where you are at, but learning to enjoy life where you are.   Being content is not saying that you have decided that where you are now is where you *always* want to be.

If you are satisfied, then you are saying that where you are now is where you want to stay in life.   It is saying: "I have arrived!" I no longer have to try to get better; I no longer have to work. I can sit back and relax. I like to use the example of my kids when they first entered preschool. Of course, I was happy and excited for them, but I didn't want them to spend the rest of their life in preschool. I was content in the time for where they were, but I wasn't satisfied about them ending up there forever.

There is a story about Diogenes, a Greek philosopher, that illustrates contentment perfectly. Diogenes was poor, living in a barrel that he rolled from place to place. One day he was approached by Alexander the Great, the Greek ruler who had everything a man living at that time could ever imagine wanting or having. Alexander approached Diogenes as he was lying on the ground outside of his barrel. Alexander asked Diogenes if there was anything that he could get or do for the philosopher, to which Diogenes simply said, "you can step aside a little as not to keep the sunshine from me." To that, the king turned to his officers and said, "If I were not Alexander, I should like to be Diogenes." That is *contentment.*

Everybody Makes Mistakes. It's okay to make mistakes. In fact, if you lived a life in which you did everything perfectly and you never made a mistake, it would probably be a very boring existence. Mistakes are a part of life. Instead of running and hiding from them, *embrace* them. Use your mistakes as learning experiences. Whatever you do, don't become negative or self-critical about your mistakes. I know many people who spend a great deal of time putting themselves down, or being overly self-critical for past mistakes. I believe that people who do this are trying to avoid criticism by *other* people. They may think, "Hey, I should criticize myself before somebody else does." One of the most self-destructive things you can do is to berate yourself. Don't do it! If someone else criticizes you for your mistakes, who cares? Don't do it to yourself. The idea is to not continue making the same mistakes; that's insanity. Learn from them and change!

Avoid Isolation From Others. Get involved in something. Talk to people and do things that involve others. Join a club, volunteer, or just call a friend. If you don't, there's a good chance that you are isolating yourself from other people. It's easy to go to work, come home and turn on the television. Yes, you probably did have a hard day at work. I won't disagree; and you probably socialized with people there too. The problem with that line of reasoning is, that most of the socializing you did at work, was probably about work. You need to spend time interacting with people who have common interests. I call them friends. I know that you probably tolerate or maybe even like your cubicle mate or work partner, but it is very unlikely that you are getting the interaction that you need, at a personal level, from work.

Isolation *allows* deceptive thinking about the world, other people and yourself. When you spend a great deal of time isolating, your thoughts begin to be led and directed by your pride and ego. If you don't share these thoughts with others, there is no one to *challenge* them. Unchallenged thoughts are usually negative. You simply begin to think things that are false and sometimes dangerous. Don't confuse isolation with taking quiet time or personal time; these are good, but taking them to the extreme, leads to isolation which is damaging.

Have Reasonable Expectations. For years I would get into a rut when the seasons changed from winter to spring. Living in New England with all of the winter weather, when the calendar said spring, I would usually be ready for spring. I would be excited for the warm weather and sunny days. The chance to get outside and enjoy nature would occupy my mind. Then it would happen. It would rain and snow. It would be cold and cloudy.

I would never understand this, until I realized, that it wasn't that spring had disappointed me, just like last year. It was my expectations that were wrong, not the season. Just because I put an "X" on the calendar for the first day of spring, does not mean that everything suddenly changed overnight.

Gradually, day after day, it would get warmer and the wind would ease. The snow showers would become fewer and farther between. It would get warmer, nicer and more pleasant outside, as my expectations stayed reasonable. Before I knew it, I was complaining about how hot and humid it was outside.

Learn To Make Good Decisions. If you are still making the same mistakes today, that you did 5, 10 or even 15 years ago, you need to seek wisdom in your life and your decision making process. The best way to acquire wisdom is to pray and read the Book of Proverbs daily. Proverbs contains much information for the person honestly seeking wisdom.

Here are some guidelines to help you in your decision making process:

1. **Never make a permanent decision based on temporary circumstances.** Don't sell your snow shovels because it's 85 degrees in the middle of July. It will get cold and snowy again, if you live in the right climate.

2. **Make sure you consider all of your options before you make a decision.** Weigh all of your options carefully before committing yourself. There may be a better course of action.

3. **Consider the consequences of your decisions versus other possible courses of action**. Yes, you probably could go to happy hour with the guys from work on your way home, but did you promise your son or daughter that you would spend time with them when you got home?

4. **"Sleep on it" before you make a final decision.** Unless it's an emergency that needs your immediate action, (no that car salesman sitting across the desk, with the pen in hand is not an emergency) take it home and allow yourself time to think and do the right thing.

5. **Make sure your decision is being made based on logic and judgment, not blind emotion.** "When dealing with people, remember that you are not dealing with creatures of logic, but creatures of emotion.[34]

6. **Have a mentor and *use* them.** It doesn't need to be a professional, just find someone who is getting the results you want in life and talk to them on a regular basis. It's good to have someone to bounce stuff off of before making big decisions, if only to get a second point of view.

7. **Gather all necessary information and facts.** Nothing is worse than rushing into a decision to find out that you missed an important detail that would have affected your choice.

8. **Don't have wrong expectations.** If you go fishing in a rain puddle, there's a good chance your not going to catch many fish. If that's what you decide, don't be disappointed with the results.

9. **Be consistent.** Make sure other people know the types of decisions you make and try as much as possible to be consistent. You will make it easier on yourself and everyone else around you.

10. **Don't be too hard on yourself.** Growth takes time and that includes learning to make *consistently* wise choices. Even then, you will still make mistakes. Remember, you are human and are guaranteed to make wrong decisions some of the time.

See Action Step #11

Learn To Be Happy. Socrates, like most philosophers, was convinced that all people desire happiness. This country's founding fathers thought that it was important enough to mention it in The Declaration Of Independence. People have pursued it; some have found it. *Most* haven't. What is this thing called happiness and how do you achieve it?

Dictionary.com defines happiness as: 1) the quality or state of being happy; 2) good fortune; pleasure; contentment; joy.

I believe that happiness is the measure we place on our current situation in life. It is how we evaluate our present circumstances that determines if we are happy or not. It's amazing how some people can "have it all" and still be miserable. It's just as amazing, though, how some people can lose "everything" and still maintain their happiness.

So, what is the difference between these two extremes and how can *you* learn to be happy, no matter what is going on in your life?

These are the characteristics that I have found to be present in the lives of people that I have met who seem to be happy. While the unhappy people tend to lack them:

- **Faith:** I see the benefits of faith time and time again. In fact, it has been mentioned many times throughout these principles. There is a reason! People with faith *know* that things will get better, so they have a reason for hope if their present circumstances are less than perfect. Study after study proves that people with faith are far happier than people without.

- **Meaningful Work:** Proverbs 12:14 states "From the fruit of his lips a man is filled with good things as surely as the work of his hands rewards him." You need to find work that not only satisfies you, but also helps others. When you know that you have helped someone and made their existence here in our world better you will be happy. You don't necessarily have to find a new job, or begin a new career, to find meaningful work. Meaningful work can be *anything* that you are currently doing. Just make sure you're benefiting those around you. Whether they are co-workers, customers or clients, make them better for having interacted with you. That is meaningful work!

- **Generosity:** Generous people are happy. They give out of the *abundance* of their heart. I don't know if generous people give because they are happy, or that people that give are happy because they are generous. I just know that there *is* a connection. So learn to be generous. Remember that it's not just about money. Give of your time, talent, energy, wisdom, faith, knowledge, etc. "Remember this: Whoever sows sparingly will also reap sparingly, and whoever sows generously will also reap generously. Each of you should give what you have decided in your heart to give, not reluctantly or under compulsion, for God loves a cheerful giver. And God is able to bless you abundantly, so that in all things at all times, having all that you need, you will abound in every good work."[35]

- **Family:** The people who are in our lives on a continual basis; those who stick with us, when everyone else ditches us, are the people who matter. Yes, they may make us angry sometimes and our pride and ego may cause some friction, but these are the people who make life worth living. Make sure that you are giving to your family relationships *more* than taking away and you will always feel that very real blessing of happiness.

- **Friends:** Having friends to share our blessings with is very important for our overall level of happiness. Friends are people who share similar interests and have similar hobbies. It may be a spiritual group, people we know from the gym, or a fantasy football league. These are the people who can help round out our lives and allow us to have some fun and recreation. Just don't spread yourself *too* thin in this area, or you will find yourself more stressed than relaxed. Remember, you are looking for quality not quantity in your friendships.

- **Husband/Wife:** Your husband or wife *should* be your most significant source of happiness. They *should* be your best friend and in some cases, even a business partner, as in my case. They *should* be the person that you can share your secrets, fears, wants, desires, shortcomings and mistakes with. They *should* be someone who you trust in all circumstances and in all situations. They *should* be the person who you desire to spend the most time with and you should follow through on actually spending that time with them. He or she is the one you will spend your life with. If this is not the case in your life, I urge you to fix this problem the best you can or you will be missing out on a very important aspect of happiness. "The husband should fulfill his marital duty to his wife, and likewise the wife to her husband. The wife does not have authority over her own body but yields it to her husband. In the same way, the husband does not have authority over his own body but yields it to his wife."[36]

See Action Step #12

Communication With God

This is a very *important* aspect of communication, but people rarely think about it as actual communication. The actual time spent with God or not spent with God has a profound effect on our lives. I will not be talking about it here, in this fundamental, except to stress the importance of this activity. I will, however, talk about it in other areas of this program. Did I mention how *important* it is?

Conclusion

The communication that you engage in or fail to engage in, impacts *every* area of your life. Learn to constantly improve in all areas of communication and you will reap the benefits. I will end on this thought: "You have it easily in your power to increase the sum total of this world's happiness now. How? By giving a few words of sincere appreciation to someone who is lonely or discouraged. Perhaps you will forget tomorrow the kind words you say today, but the recipient may cherish them over a lifetime."[37]

Summary

- Communication Basics
- Some Suggestions About Communication
- Would You Rather Be Right Or Happy?
- Ten Rules For Communication
  - Speak The Truth In Love
  - Speak Life
  - Speak Empowerment
  - Speak Positively
  - Speak Forgiveness
  - Speak Praise
  - Be Kinder Than Necessary
  - Never Say But
  - Take Off The Mask
  - Listen
- Three questions to ask yourself before you say anything
- Communication and Learning Styles
  - Visual
  - Auditory
  - Feeling Oriented
- Communication With Your Family
  - Communication With Your Husband or Wife
  - Communication With Your Children
  - Stages of Development
    - The Beginning Years
    - The Searching Years
    - The "Real" World
- Discipline Your Kids
- Communication with Yourself
  - Be Content, Not Satisfied
  - Everybody Makes Mistakes
  - Avoid Isolation From Others
  - Have Reasonable Expectations
  - Learn To Make Good Decisions
  - Learn To Be Happy
- Communication With God

Prayer for Communication

Lord, guide my words today. Help me to communicate in the right way, at the right time to the right people.

Amen.

Action Steps for Communication

Communication Action Step 1 – Compliments & Criticism

In this Action Step you are going to learn to compliment when you need to criticize. Start TODAY giving 5 compliments for every criticism.

Do the following activities:

1. Who may you have to criticize today? Why?

    _____

    _____

    _____

    _____

    _____

2. What are 5 compliments you can give that person?

    _____

    _____

    _____

3. What are your thoughts, ideas and feelings about compliments and criticism:

    _____

    _____

    _____

    _____

    _____

    _____

    _____

    _____

    _____

    _____

    _____

Communication Action Step 2 – Effective Communication

In this Action Step you are going to practice the Ten Rules of Communication. Review them starting on page 94. Use as many of these rules as you can in every conversation you have today.

Record your results here:

1. What rules did you follow?

_____

_____

_____

2. What rules do you need to work on?

_____

_____

_____

3. What are your thoughts, ideas and feelings about effective communication?

_____

_____

_____

_____

_____

_____

Communication Action Step 3 – Three Questions

In this Action Step you are going to begin asking yourself these three questions before you say anything.

For today make these 3 questions part of your thinking

- Does it need to be said?
- Does it need to be said now?
- Does it need to be said now by you?

Do the following activities:

1. Did you ask yourself these 3 questions before speaking today?

   _____

   _____

   _____

2. Think of one instance when asking yourself these questions helped. How did they help you?

   _____

   _____

   _____

3. What are your thoughts, ideas and feelings about these three questions?

   _____

   _____

   _____

Communication Action Step 4 –Communication & Learning Styles

In your interactions with other people today find at least one person with each of the communication styles.

Answer these questions:

1. Who did you interact with today that fell into each of the 3 communication & learning styles?

    _____

    _____

    _____

2. How were your experiences with each of them different?

    _____

    _____

    _____

3. What is your communication and learning style? How do you know?

    _____

    _____

    _____

4. What are your thoughts, ideas and feelings about communication and learning styles?

    _____

    _____

    _____

Communication Action Step 5 – Eat Together

In this Action Step you are going to create a plan to make sure you are eating at least one meal a day with your family.

Do the following activities:

1. What is one thing you can do today to ensure you will eat at least one meal with your family every day?

   _____

   _____

   _____

2. What meal will you eat with them? What time will it be?

   _____

   _____

   _____

3. What are some positive topics of conversation that can be discussed? Do they include everybody?

   _____

   _____

   _____

4. What are your thoughts, ideas and feelings about eating together?

   _____

   _____

   _____

Communication Action Step 6 – Practicing Acceptance

In this Action Step you are going to begin the practice of acceptance towards everyone in your family.

Do the following activities:

1. What is every family member's favorite food? When will you have it?

    _____

    _____

    _____

2. List every family member's favorite activity and do it this week. Also do it every week from now on. When will you start?

    _____

    _____

    _____

    _____

3. Find an activity that everyone likes, that you can all do together. Write the activity below. When will you do this?

    _____

    _____

    _____

4. For the activities listed in numbers 2 and 3, commit to the time when you will do these activities. Write it down.

    _____

    _____

    _____

    _____

5. What are your thoughts, ideas and feelings about practicing acceptance?

_____

_____

_____

_____

_____

_____

_____

_____

_____

_____

_____

_____

_____

_____

_____

_____

_____

_____

_____

_____

_____

_____

_____

_____

Communication Action Step 7 –
Communication With Your Spouse

In this Action Step you are going to improve your communication with your spouse. Do something nice for your husband or wife today. Make it something unexpected. Base it on their communication and learning style, if possible.

Do the following activities:

1. What did you do? When?

   _____

   _____

   _____

2. How did he/she respond?

   _____

   _____

   _____

3. What can you do tomorrow?

   _____

   _____

   _____

4. What are your thoughts, ideas and feelings about communicating with your spouse?

   _____

   _____

   _____

   _____

   _____

   _____

Communication Action Step 8 – Overcoming A "Generational Curse"

In this Action Step you are going to overcome a "generational curse" that is hurting your life and may be passed on to your children.

Do these activities:

1. List one "generational curse" that has had a negative impact on your life.

    _____

    _____

    _____

2. How do you plan on breaking it?

    _____

    _____

    _____

3. What is something you can do right now to break it? When will you do this?

    _____

    _____

    _____

4. What are your thoughts, ideas and feelings about overcoming generational curses?

    _____

    _____

    _____

Communication Action Step 9 – Teach Your Kids

In this Action Step you will begin the process of teaching your kids the lessons they will need for success.

Talk to your kids today and do the following activities:

1. How will you empower your kids?

_____

_____

_____

2. What will you teach your kids about the world?

_____

_____

_____

3. What will you teach your kids about God?

_____

_____

_____

4. When will you begin this process?

_____

_____

_____

5. What are your thoughts, ideas and feelings about teaching your kids?

_____

_____

_____

Communication Action Step 10 – Lessons Learned

In this Action Step you are going to examine the lessons you learned as a child (both negative and positive) and discover where you can change the negative and strengthen the positive. To begin, review the lists of negative and positive lessons beginning on page 91.

Then do the following activities:

1. What negative lessons from the list did you learn as a child?

    _____

    _____

    _____

2. What negative lessons did you learn that are not included on the list?

    _____

    _____

    _____

3. What positive lessons from the list did you learn as a child?

    _____

    _____

    _____

4. What positive lessons did you learn that are not included on the list?

    _____

    _____

    _____

5. What can you do, today, to change the negative of the past and strengthen and positive?

    _____

    _____

    _____

6. What are your thoughts, ideas and feelings about the negative and positive lessons you have learned?

    _____

    _____

    _____

Communication Action Step 11 – Making Good Decisions

In this Action Step you are going to learn how to make good decisions. Review the section titled "Learn To Make Good Decisions" starting on page 94.

Then do the following activities:

1. Think of an important decision you made recently. What was it?

   _____

   _____

   _____

2. Which of the guidelines did you follow well in making your decision?

   _____

   _____

   _____

3. Which of the guidelines do you need to work on?

   _____

   _____

   _____

   _____

   _____

   _____

   _____

4. What are your thoughts, ideas and feelings about making good decisions?

   _____

   _____

   _____

Communication Action Step 12 – Learn To Be Happy

In this Action Step you are going to practice being happy. Review the section titled, "Learn To Be Happy," starting on page 96.

Do the following activities:

1. Write a short paragraph about what it takes to make you happy. How many suggestions from this section are included?

_____

_____

_____

2. Which of the suggestions are you doing well at?

_____

_____

_____

3. Which of the suggestions do you need to work on?

_____

_____

_____

4. What are your thoughts, ideas and feelings about learning to be happy?

_____

_____

_____

_____

_____

The Principle of Generosity

A Candle is not dimmed by lighting
another candle. – Unknown

A generous man will prosper; he who refreshes others
will himself be refreshed. Proverbs 11:25 (NIV)

What Is Generosity?

When people think about the topic of generosity what usually comes to mind is money. More specifically, *their* money and what *they* need to give away. Generosity certainly includes money and how much of your money you give away to help others. That is only a small part of generosity though.

Yes, generosity is much more than giving away money. Generosity is about time, talent, knowledge, wisdom, faith and just about anything else that you may possess. In fact, you are very unlikely to become financially successful unless you learn to be generous in *all* areas of your life.

Generosity, when practiced without restraint, bears fruit that improves the life of the receiver as well as the giver. I have seen countless lives (including mine) turned around by the spirit of giving. In order to reap the benefits of generosity, it must be practiced with no thought or intention of gaining anything. "Do all the good you can; by all the means you can, in all the ways you can, in all the places you can, at all the times you can, to all the people you can, as long as you ever can."[38]

Generosity is more than dropping ten dollars in the offering plate at church on Christmas Eve. It is more than financial. It is giving of your time, energy, talents, and strengths. It is finding how you can serve most effectively and then acting on that. It is giving up comforts in order for someone else to live.

Practicing generosity in *every* area of life, leads to unimaginable success. Find where you can be generous today and do it. You will have a sense of belonging and fulfillment that you never dreamed of. A floodgate of good things will be opened to you and you won't be able to contain the goodness that will flow into your life (as long as that's not your motivation behind the generosity). Try it today and see how your life changes. "Give generously to them and do so without a grudging heart; then because of this the LORD your God will bless you in all your work and in everything you put your hand to."[39]

Generosity's Starting Point

Generosity is a characteristic that will *always* lead to success, in every area of your life. Like anything worth having though, it must be strengthened and developed every day. When you learn to give of your time, talent, energy and money, you will begin to experience success in *all* areas of your life.

A good place to start being generous is with *yourself*. Many people don't realize this, but if you can't be nice to yourself, how are you going to develop the quality of generosity that brings value to *everyone* else? Practice giving yourself more time to relax, or buy yourself something nice when you have achieved an objective that you have set. Practice developing the self-worth necessary to accept these gifts for yourself without feeling guilty. Simply allow yourself to receive from others, yourself and God. Once you are able to give to yourself, you become better equipped to handle the challenge that learning to be generous with others creates.

See Action Step #1

Your ability to be generous is *directly* related to knowing your direction in life and whether you are successful or not. You must know where you're headed and why. I have found that someone who is not generating success will not be a very generous giver. If they're not sure where they may end up in twenty years, they will not share their time, talent, energy and money. They will fear running out of these assets in the future.

Three Types of People:

I have identified three types of people. Most people fall into one of the following categories concerning their generosity:

1. Takers

2. Keepers

3. Givers

I have also seen the effects of these particular lifestyles on the results people get in *all* areas of life. "The person who plants selfishness, ignoring the needs of others - ignoring God - harvests a crop of weeds. All he'll have to show for his life is weeds! But the one who plants in response to God, letting God's spirit do the growth work in him, harvests a crop of real life, eternal life."[40]

For the most part, people are neither takes nor givers, but keepers. I will describe these three types of people and you will decide where you fall in. Of course, these are generalizations and most people fall somewhere between two categories.

Takers: We all know at least a few *takers*. These are the people who are always "allowing" other people to do nice things for them, but are never available when someone else needs help. A good example of a taker is someone who gathers all of their friends together to help them move into a new apartment, but when one of those friends needs help they are too busy.

A great illustration of takers is the Pharaohs of ancient Egypt. The Pharaohs believed that their spirits would remain in their bodies after they died. They would then set out on their passage into the hereafter. Because of this belief, they expended large amounts of their kingdom's resources to make sure their passage would be pleasant and safe.

Many of the Pharaohs began to establish their plans for this transition as their first priority upon taking the throne. They forced tens of thousands of their own people into years of harsh and grueling work so that *they* would be preserved.

Building pyramids was not easy. It is thought to have taken over twenty thousand workers about 80 years to build the Pyramids at Giza. The workers were required to move stones averaging 2.5 tons out of rock quarries and across the desert. This was all done without modern tools and equipment, of course.

The main purpose of the pyramids was to protect the Pharaoh's body after death. The body itself was worked on for over two months with embalmers working to preserve it for burial. This was a further drain on the resources of the kingdom. Once finished, the mummified body was placed in an elaborately designed coffin and placed in the specially designed chamber of the pyramid.

Many historians believe that this massive use of resources was responsible for the decline and eventual failure of ancient Egypt. Spending on this overwhelming scale, of both money and other resources, left many Egyptians living in poverty and most likely destroyed the economy.

This was an ultimate act of selfishness so that the pharaoh could "preserve" himself regardless of the consequences it caused everyone else. This, of course, is a very extreme example, but many people today live only for themselves.

Keepers: The next group of people we are going to discuss are *keepers*. Just as the name suggests, they don't take from others or society, but they don't contribute anything either. Most keepers are neither stingy nor generous. They receive many things from others such as: information, faith, knowledge, money, and just about anything else you can imagine, but that's just where it stops. They never realize that the blessings in life occur when they freely pass along that which they have received from others. These people never realize that "we make a living by what we get, but we make a life by what we give."[41]

Most keepers probably don't even realize what they are doing. Sadly, this is the category that most of society falls into. With all the pressures of the day, most people spend their time working; earning a living for *themselves*. They don't have the ability to give of their time and talent; they are tired. When it comes to money, they are barely paying their bills; many times, ending up with more month at the end of their money. The same holds true for every other area of their life; they just can't give. Of course, this belief is complete nonsense.

Many keepers are also what I like to call, "score keepers." They pay very close attention to the generosity others extend to them and tend to repay the same amount of generosity back to those who give. Also, when they are generous with other people, they keep track of what they have already given, making sure they receive the same amount back.

The sad thing about keepers is that they just don't understand or comprehend that in order to have more they must give more. Unlike takers, who are usually acting out of their own greed, selfishness and fear, keepers tend to misunderstand the laws of sowing and reaping. Many times these people want to do well, but they haven't been shown how.

Givers: The last group of people is *givers*. These are the people who give without any thought of getting anything in return. They have discovered that true success comes from giving and helping. They understand that by giving away what they have, they will be given more. It is an upward cycle of generosity that leads to unimaginable contentment and success.

The most famous of all givers was Mother Teresa, who said, "Let no one ever come to you without leaving better and happier. Be the living expression of God's kindness: kindness in your face, kindness in your eyes, kindness in your smile."[42]

We have all heard of Mother Teresa, but many of us don't know the extent of her generous heart. She is the perfect example of a giver; something we should all strive for in our own lives.

Mother Teresa was the founder of the order of the Missionaries Of Charity. This is an organization dedicated to helping the poor and destitute of India.

She started this organization in 1948 after teaching at a school for the privileged for over 15 years.

In 1946, then Sister Teresa began sensing God's call on her life, which was to give herself to caring for India's poor. She moved to the slums and committed herself to the work that she was called to do.

With little in the way of resources, little by little, she began to make a difference. Soon, others began to come to help her. Before long, schools were formed and medical care began being administered to the poor.

Throughout the years, her group was responsible for building a hospice, where the terminally ill could die with dignity. They opened centers that served the blind, the disabled and the elderly. They also built a leper colony.

By the time of her death in 1997, the organization she founded had grown to include operations in over 90 countries. There were over 4,000 nuns and hundreds of thousands of volunteers and other workers.

Mother Teresa understood these words: "Do not store up for yourselves treasures on earth, where moths and vermin destroy, and where thieves break in and steal. But store up for yourselves treasures in heaven, where moths and vermin do not destroy, and where thieves do not break in and steal. For where your treasure is, there your heart will be also."[43]

The Two Seas In Israel

It is obvious that those who give more, naturally receive more, but why?

I like to use an example comparing the Sea of Galilee and the Dead Sea to illustrate why this is so. Imagine, for a moment, that the Dead Sea represents both *takers* and *keepers*. Imagine also, that the Sea of Galilee represents *givers*.

If you were to observe the Dead Sea, you would notice that the scenery is ugly. The atmosphere is harsh and the shores are barren. The water is not able to sustain life and cannot quench thirst.

Looking at the Sea of Galilee, we discover an entirely different situation. The scenery is beautiful. The atmosphere is pleasant and the water, as well as the shore, is fertile. The water is full of sea creatures. The area surrounding it is full of productive farmland and thriving villages.

So what causes this vast difference? The difference, I believe, is in the giving.

The Dead Sea (takers and keepers), receives a reliable and continuous flow of fresh water. The water that flows into its shores stays there. It is kept. The abundance of minerals that flow into it from the Jordan River is kept within its limits.

The Sea of Galilee also receives a reliable and continuous flow of fresh water. The water flows in from the mountains located to the north. The difference is that this sea freely supplies the Jordan River with its abundance.

The sea that remains full of life and prospers is the one that gives its abundance away. It is a source of richness, because it freely gives its riches away.

People are the same way. We can only prosper by the prosperity we spread into other people's lives. When you give out your resources, you will receive even more to give. You will be full of abundance and life, just like the Sea of Galilee.

King Solomon said, "The world of the generous gets larger and larger; the world of the stingy gets smaller and smaller. The one who blesses others is abundantly blessed; those who help others are helped."[44] How true!

See Action Step #2

Taking It One Step Further

Even if you *are* a giver, it takes more than just giving stuff away to reap the benefits of generosity. This is where even the most generous givers can go wrong.

It is a matter of attitude about giving that determines the level at which you will reap. I have determined that there are two types of givers; they are cheerful givers and grudging givers. We know that there are many people who fall somewhere in the middle of the spectrum of these two extremes, but for illustration purposes we will focus on these two.

The cheerful giver is *happy* to part with his or her resources and help wherever they see the need. Not only do these people tithe at church, but they also contribute their other resources such as time, talent, knowledge, etc. when they see a need. This is a win/win situation.

The grudging giver, on the other hand, may do the same giving, but it is usually with an attitude of expecting something in return. Even worse, they may harbor resentments because of all that they are "required" to do. This is a situation where they benefit others but not themselves, a win/lose situation.

It's easy to see the difference. In fact, "...Whoever sows sparingly will also reap sparingly, and whoever sows generously will also reap generously. Each of you should give what you have decided in your heart to give, not reluctantly or under compulsion, for God loves a cheerful giver. And God is able to bless you abundantly, so that in all things at all times, having all that you need, you will abound in every good work."[45]

Thankfully, we get to *decide* whether we will be takers, keepers or givers. When we decide to be givers, we are creating lasting relationships, in which we are the catalyst for positive results in *everybody's* life that we encounter, including our own. We are making a difference that will outlive us, while at the same time strengthening our relationships with God, other people and ourselves.

So what are you? Are you a taker? Keeper? Giver? It is interesting to find out. It's only when we uncover who we are that we can move forward into becoming a cheerful giver. If you already are a giver, work at becoming even *more* generous.

See Action Step #3.

You Can Make a Difference

If you have *decided* to live your life as a giver, then let me take the time to congratulate you. Life is going to take on new meaning and you will begin to have an impact on your world in ways you may never have imagined. I have experienced this changed existence and know how great it is.

There are *many* types of needs; the needs of the world are huge. In fact, when we look around, we see an infinite amount of need, very little of which is actually being met. Besides the obvious needs to supply our less fortunate fellow humans with the basic necessities, I have found these needs:

- The need for peace in areas where there is now war.
- The need for food and clothing in third world countries.
- The need for strong friendships and families.
- The need for jobs, tuition and a new car.
- The need for belonging and purpose.
- The need for...the list is *endless*.

The Need For God

One of our world's *greatest* needs is the ability and desire to share God. In order for you to take hold of all that generosity has to offer, you must share God with *every* person you encounter. *"Go into all the world and preach the gospel to all creation."*[46] I am not talking about pushing your beliefs on others, which will actually have the opposite effect on people than what you should be striving for. Don't be pushy! Simply learn to share by the life you lead. Share by example! Live your life in such a way that people *see* the positive results you achieve. They will take note of it and that's when they will begin to ask questions.

Just taking a look at the current state of our world should be enough to convince anybody of the need to share God. We live in a world that has become overcome by materialism, greed, corruption and immorality. People simply cannot keep up at the expense of the important things in our lives such as love, health, achievement and real success. I believe that people are searching, like never before, for peace. They are looking for peace that can't be achieved by material possessions, money in your bank account, power or decadence.

This emptiness has often led people to search for answers in the occult or new age philosophies, leading to even more emptiness. I have found that this cycle can be broken by you!

Without your generosity, in sharing God, many people will die without getting to know Him and the joy that comes with this relationship. More importantly, they will not get the opportunity to spend eternity with Him, in heaven.

We have *all* sinned. In fact, "...all have sinned and fall short of the glory of God..."[47] Some of us have found new life in this program. If that describes you, then it is your responsibility to help others find their spiritual footing.

If you decide to do nothing, friends, relatives, neighbors and even close family members such as: children, spouses and parents may be lost *forever*. Nobody is doing anything to help them and they are slipping further and further away from the truth. They are grasping at anything that may offer the illusion of hope. I was at a relative's house recently and there, sitting on the coffee table was a psychic healing book. If you look around, the reality of the situation hits close to home.

Don't be someone who is afraid to stand out and stand upon the truth. If we look at the condition of the world today, we will see that many people have lost faith and focus. They have become disillusioned, in many cases rightfully so, into thinking that church is nothing more than a social club.

As a result of life pressures, they have become burdened by other people's responsibilities and have lost their way. Even people, who may have developed a strong sense of spirituality and great relationship with God in the past, may need help. This happens mainly for two reasons:

1. They begin to develop a spiritual lifestyle, but things don't happen quickly enough for them, so they fall away.

2. They begin to develop a spiritual lifestyle but begin acting dumb and irresponsible in their choices and actions thereby they push people away.

So the question I ask is why isn't the challenge of sharing God being met? I believe it comes down to five main reasons and if you haven't been generous with sharing God, then it is probably because of one of these:

Lack of concern: In our self-centered world, many people have become more concerned with themselves than they are with helping anyone else. They are not concerned for God, even though He has done so much for us.[48] They are not concerned for others, even though concern and care for others is precisely what will help them grow in spirituality.[49] They are not concerned for themselves, failing to realize that they must help others if they, themselves are to be helped.[50]

Are you concerned?

Lack of knowledge: Many people simply lack knowledge of God's word. They don't believe or realize that God has called *them*[51]. Furthermore, they do not allow themselves to be taught, so they can teach others.[52] Many times they simply do not know how to act. They do not know that being *themselves* will allow God to put the people in their path that *they* can help. Be honest and real!

Are you willing to take a chance?

Lack of courage: We all have fears. Some common fears that we experience include being rejected by loved ones, ridiculed by friends and criticized by society. There is no need to fear these things. If you are being rejected, ridiculed or criticized for Jesus, then you are blessed. ""Blessed are you when people insult you, persecute you and falsely say all kinds of evil against you because of me. Rejoice and be glad, because great is your reward in heaven, for in the same way they persecuted the prophets who were before you."[53]

Remember that you are trying to please God, not people. "Am I now trying to win the approval of human beings, or of God? Or am I trying to please people? If I were still trying to please people, I would not be a servant of Christ."[54]

Are you willing to be brave?

Lack of Faith: Some people don't believe that God's word is true. They don't believe it when it describes what results from sin. "For the wages of sin is death, but the gift of God is eternal life in Christ Jesus our Lord."[55]

There are others who don't believe God's word is true, when it describes the world and our relationship to it. Some people do not believe God's ability to give us strength, wisdom and courage. It is clear that, "I can do everything through Him who gives me strength."[56]

Are you willing to stand in faith?

Lack of Focus: Many times people become distracted by things of the world. They focus too much on the world's rules of success and happiness. Before long, "...as they go on their way they are choked by life's worries, riches and pleasures, and they do not mature."[57]

You must decide what you will devote your life to. You cannot love God *and* the world. "Do not love the world or anything in the world. If anyone loves the world, love for the Father is not in them. For everything in the world—the lust of the flesh, the lust of the eyes, and the pride of life—comes not from the Father but from the world. The world and its desires pass away, but whoever does the will of God lives forever."[58]

It's also important to note, that you cannot "...serve two masters. Either you will hate the one and love the other, or you will be devoted to the one and despise the other. You cannot serve both God and money."[59]

So, are you willing to focus on God's will for your life?

Sharing God is *the most important area to be generous in*. It is part of God's plan and you must share in this area, if you are to have any type of success at all. Why?

This is what we are told to do[60]. It also shows that we care about other people[61]. In addition, the most important reason to share God's word is to help save other people. By doing this, you are sharing in the joy of heaven. "Count on it—there's more joy in heaven over one sinner's rescued life than over ninety-nine good people in no need of rescue."[62] I have seen in my own life, the incredible fulfillment and success that comes from sharing His word.[63]

See Action Step #4

The *biggest* need in the world today, is for people to share the word of God. The best way to do this is to become a worker in His kingdom. Don't count yourself among the people, who through attitudes and actions have produced a lack of concern, knowledge, courage, faith and focus.

So what can you do? If you are asking this question of yourself, then you are concerned. Here is the short answer:

- Become knowledgeable...learn.

- Become courageous...pray.

- Become strong in your faith...act.

- Become focused...plan.

You Will Harvest What You Plant

This rule of generosity is quite simple, yet many times it seems to be overlooked by most people. "Do not be deceived: God cannot be mocked. A man reaps what he sows. Whoever sows to please their flesh, from the flesh will reap destruction; whoever sows to please the Spirit, from the Spirit will reap eternal life. Let us not become weary in doing good, for at the proper time we will reap a harvest if we do not give up. Therefore, as we have opportunity, let us do good to all people..."[64]

Many people don't believe that the law of sowing and reaping works. There are those who will mock this truth. We live in a period where people are so interested in *themselves* that they refuse to look at the evidence.

The evidence is this: sowing and reaping produce a harvest of *many* blessings for those who embrace it! Many people find it hard to believe that God will bless those who do well. Some people even try to convince others to turn their backs on what they think is an absurd idea.

Many people who struggle with allowing blessings to flow into their lives, struggle with this concept. When they allow doubt or disbelief into their minds, they unknowingly refuse to allow the law of sowing and reaping to work in their lives in a positive manner. I know of many people who have refused these promises and have walked away from generosity all together.

Many times, negative attitudes about sowing and reaping begin after someone has actually tried applying this law in their own life. They may have tried it for a *short* time and didn't get the results they thought they deserved. Sadly, the practice was abandoned and they now act as though sowing and reaping doesn't produce positive results. They go around trying to convince others that sowing and reaping doesn't work. They may even mock those who obey this law.

Most people relate the law of sowing and reaping to finances and money, but this rule applies to *any* area of life. "Good will come to him who is generous and lends freely, who conducts his affairs with justice."[65] This rule applies to work, love, time, health, kindness, patience, friendship, forgiveness and more. It also works with negative forces as well. If you sow hatred, greed, bitterness, negativity or any other negative force, you will reap that in your life. All of these things are seeds that you may be sowing.

In another version of Galatians 6:7 it says "whatsoever."[66] Think about this, it means <u>whatsoever</u> or everything someone sows, will produce a harvest. This is simply a law of God that applies to *every* area of our lives. There are no exceptions!

A farmer does not just go out one day and start harvesting crops. I know from experience, that in the garden in my backyard, I do not simply go out in the summer and start picking tomatoes. First, I need to plant the seeds. Next, I need to water and weed the garden. Then after a season, if I am diligent, I begin to see the harvest. It's the same with any area of your life. Consistent good will not come, unless it is *first* sown into the world.

It's important to note that we are not talking about a one-time event here. You do not sow one day and then the following day begin to reap a harvest. No, you must *continually* sow. It takes time. You must learn to sow, day after day, week after week, and year after year. It must be made a habit, so that if you don't do it, something inside of you doesn't feel quite right. If you are faithful, steady and habitual in your sowing, you will reap a harvest...<u>guaranteed</u>. It's a *promise* of God that, "he who gives to the poor will lack nothing, but he who closes his eyes to them receives many curses."[67]

The biggest reason so many people walk away from sowing and reaping is because they never really gave it a chance. They may have sown a few times; they may even have had a genuine heart when doing it. They may have even waited patiently for a day, or a month and their harvest didn't materialize. When nothing happened, they lost interest.

The key is to realize that the level in which you reap is in direct proportion to what you sow into other people's lives and the world. In other words, if you sow a little, then you will reap a little. If you sow a lot, then you will also reap a lot. If you sow occasionally, then you will reap occasionally. Sow consistently and you will reap consistently. If you learn to make sowing a habit, that is practiced regularly, then that is exactly what you will reap in your life.

Remember that you are producing a harvest and it doesn't happen overnight. If you are working at planting positive seeds in the lives of others, you will reap a harvest if you do not give up.[68] Your harvest will come at the *proper* time. Depending on the climate of a particular region, harvest times may be different for growers.   In Florida, for instance, they begin harvest much sooner than growers in Maine.

Never Stop Giving

The point I am trying to make is that you should *never* stop giving. You may hear other people talking about how giving "doesn't work."   You may begin to think these thoughts yourself. You may even reach a point, where you begin to reason that you don't have to give so much or that you have been giving long enough and deserve something. If you allow yourself to adopt that pattern of thinking and begin to ease up on your giving, then all of your previous generosity would have been in vain. Don't ever stop planting seeds of generosity and giving. I know from experience that: "The individual is capable of both great compassion and great indifference.   He has it within his means to nourish the former and outgrow the later."[69]

This law of sowing and reaping applies to *every* area of life, not just money. Sowing, good or bad, will produce the same in your life. If you want friendship in your life, then offer friendship to someone else. If you want to be forgiven, then you first must offer forgiveness; and of course, if you want money, then you must offer it generously into the lives' of other people. Remember though, it works on the negative side too. If you are spreading hatred, then that's what you will experience. If you spend time gossiping about your neighbors, you can bet that someone's gossiping about you. Everything comes back and it comes back multiplied. Just like one apple seed produces an apple tree that will return countless apples.

Many people try to deny this law, but that doesn't make the law any less real. *Whatever* you sow, no matter what it is, is what you will reap in your life. This is in fact a law of God. You can't change it, so you should learn to work with it. Decide now what you want to reap in your life.

See Action Step #5

So decide now what you want to plant in your life. If you want hardship and struggle, don't do good for other people. If you want success and abundance, do good wherever you can. As Albert Einstein once said, "The value of a man should be seen in what he gives and not what he is able to receive."[70]

Tithing

Tithing, put simply, is taking the *first* ten percent of your income and sowing it into God's kingdom. In other words, it's giving ten percent of your money to your church.

Tithing is discussed in the Principle Of Money. Just to remind you, tithing is *required*! If you can't follow this simple rule, how are you supposed to be responsible enough to handle real financial success? If you follow through on this, with the right attitude and give out of the spirit of your heart, you will receive financial blessing in great abundance. God says, "Bring the whole tithe into the store house, that there may be food in my house. Test me in this," says the Lord Almighty, "and see if I will not throw open the floodgates of heaven and pour out so much blessing that you will not have room enough for it."[71]

Generosity Above Tithing

Before going any further, you must determine *who* your source of abundance is. This comes down to three choices: you, other people or God. Unfortunately, most people live their life as if the answer is either number one or number two or a combination of both. Most people don't realize that it is number three. It is God!

By admitting that God is the source of abundance in your life, you are acknowledging three things:

1. Everything belongs to Him.

2. He can provide for you.

3. You need to be a good steward of everything He has entrusted to you.

Being Generous Without Spending A lot Of Money

A discussion of generosity always comes back to spending money and material things. So, I am going to discuss those things now. It is important to note, however, that there are infinitely many ways to be generous and spread good. We will discuss these later in this principle. "For the love of money is the root of all evil which: which while some coveted after, they have erred from the faith, and pierced themselves through with many sorrows."[72]

It is what you *do* with money that determines how God views it. A hundred dollars that is used to feed a poor family has a different value than a hundred dollars used to feed a drug habit. Money simply makes you more of what you already were before you had the money. If, before you had an abundance of money, you were generous, then an abundance of money will make you generous in abundance. If you were greedy, before having an abundance of money, then an abundance of money will make you greedier. Money shows where your heart really is. If you want to find out what type of person you are, then take a look at where you spend your money.

Don't let money be your guide. Just as many people have found out over the last several years in the stock market, you could have lots of money one day; then the next day be in the pits of poverty. Money can't give you love or strength. Don't look to money for what only *God* can give you.

"Love of money" does not apply *just* to people who have, but also to those who lack it. You can be in the depths of poverty and have more greed than a billionaire.

If you don't have a lot of money to give above your 10%, find ways to get free stuff at the grocery stores, pharmacies and super stores (eg. Target, Wal-Mart, and others). Clipping coupons for "freebies" is a great way to give back and you're just using your time to gather the food and personal care items to give to the food bank or shelters.

Along the lines of the item above, some food banks and shelters take coupons so that they can use them when adding to their stockpiles. Donate the coupon sections from your Sunday paper; it saves them a ton of money!

Do "spring" cleaning (it doesn't really matter what season). Go through your clothes, closets, garage, pantry; figure out what you are just not using and donate it to places or people who need it and will actually use it. This act will not only benefit someone else, but it's proven that purging your life of "clutter" frees you up emotionally, physically and spiritually....less stuff, less stress!

See Action Step #6

How To Start Being Generous

Like *anything* worth having, learning to become generous is not always easy. Up to this point, you may have spent a whole lifetime seeking selfish and self-serving objectives. The best advice I can give is to be patient.

You are *ultimately* striving for a heart of generosity. Strive to do the following and you will eventually succeed: "Give to everyone who asks you, and if anyone takes what belongs to you, do not demand it back. Do to others, as you would have them do to you. If you love those who love you, what credit is that to you? Even sinners love those who love them." and "Be merciful, just as your Father is merciful. 'Do not judge, and you will not be judged. Do not condemn, and you will not be condemned. Forgive, and you will be forgiven. Give, and it will be given to you. A good measure, pressed down, shaken together and running over, will be poured into your lap. For with the measure you use, it will be measured to you.'"[73]

I have included some *practical* ideas and suggestions to help you in your desire to be generous. I suggest that you start locally. In other words, you don't need to go on a mission trip to Africa to be living in a spirit of generosity. You can *start* right where you are.

Be Neighborly: Have you ever just said 'hi' to someone passing on the street? That is where being neighborly begins.

When you learn to be friendly, you begin to create a positive environment around yourself and everyone you encounter. You are taking constructive action, which will lead to more goodwill between other people until a network of positive interactions develop.

One of the greatest joys and therefore greatest opportunities, for success, comes from shining light into places that are dark. "There are two ways of spreading light: to be the candle or the mirror that reflects it."[74]

Do Something Nice Every day: Find someone you don't know, a complete stranger, and do something nice for them. You don't have to take them out to dinner or give them a million dollars, just do *something* nice. Some examples that I like are holding the door open at the store or letting someone merge in traffic. Try going to the mall around Christmas time and simply walk in and out of the mall at different spots, holding the door open for other people. You will be surprised at people's reactions and they will be just as surprised at your generosity.

If you want to take this suggestion one step further, find someone you don't like and do nice things for *them*. Maybe you can bring a thoughtful gift to that co-worker who irritates you or move your annoying neighbor's trashcans off the road, so that traffic doesn't crush them. This is somewhat challenging but it will get easier the more you do it.

The point is, it's easy to do nice things for people we know and like. "If you love those who love you, what credit is that to you? Even sinners love those who love them. And if you do good to those who are good to you, what credit is that to you? Even sinners do that. And if you lend to those from whom you expect repayment, what credit is that to you? Even sinners lend to sinners, expecting to be repaid in full. But love your enemies, do good to them, and lend to them without expecting to get anything back. Then your reward will be great, and you will be children of the Most High, because he is kind to the ungrateful and wicked."[75]

See Action Step #7.

Experiment: We are all unique. In order for you to find a talent, ability, or gifting that you can share, you must *experiment*. Try different activities that allow you to sow goodness into other people's lives. We are not all meant to run the youth group at church or volunteer in the local soup kitchen on Thanksgiving.

You might be athletic, in which case you would be a good candidate to coach a youth sports league. Maybe you have a talent for organization, which would make you useful to many charities around Christmas time. There you would organize the incoming Christmas donations at your church or another organization. If you're good at serving, you may be able to fulfill a need at the local homeless shelter.

The point is to find your *unique* combination of talents, abilities and gifts; find out where you would be most useful.

See Action Step #8.

Share Information: You are knowledgeable about *something*. Share your knowledge with someone who may be seeking it. Don't go overboard with this by being a know it all, but be ready to help someone who may be seeking your specialized knowledge. Are you gifted in mathematics? Try volunteering in an after school program that tutors struggling teenagers. Find your gifting and use it! "The wicked borrow and do not repay, but the righteous give generously;."[76]

Sow Encouragement: We have all heard the phrase, "what goes around, comes around." This is true in many areas of life, *especially* with encouragement. I have seen the good that encouragement produces. When you help someone with kind words, it will be remembered and reciprocated when you are in need of encouragement.

Learn to be generous with encouragement and stingy with criticism. "The people who are lifting the world onward and upward are those who encourage more than they criticize."[77]

Who you become is measured, in large part, by who you attract. So if you want encouragement in your own life, make sure that you are being generous with it yourself.

See Action Step #9.

Offer Wisdom: Whether you believe it or not, you *can* be the voice of wisdom in someone else's life. You have had a set of unique experiences and life lessons that can be of use to another human being. Look for opportunities to be of help to someone who needs you. "The light which experience gives is a lantern on the stern, which shines only on the waves behind us."[78]

My only caution here is to make sure that the wisdom you are offering is true wisdom and not an opinion based on your ego. Make sure what you are offering to someone is *useful*.

You might have very specific wisdom to offer. If you are a college biology instructor, you may be able to offer wisdom that helps a struggling student about that subject. You might have wisdom that covers a broad topic, such as relationships. In this case, you may be able to offer help on many different occasions. It is important to identify areas of wisdom so that you are in a better position to help other people when the occasion arises.

Stand in Faith: Giving when you don't think you have enough, grows your faith. You cannot go and give generously one day and expect to have good things flowing into your life because of it. No, you must apply faith and continue to give, even when it *looks* as if nothing is changing in your life.

You must persist in doing good, no matter what is happening around you. "Let us not become weary in doing good, for at the proper time we will reap a harvest if we do not give up."[79]

There was a time when this point was proven in my life and I have stood upon it many times since. My wife and I have always donated to Toys for Tots, but there was one particular period where I had been out of work for over a year. We were almost out of money and saw little hope of being able to give to this organization, as we had in the past. We decided to ignore the "evidence" and give gifts to this organization anyway. We took the last of our savings and went into the toy store. We then dropped the toys off at a collection center. I received a job offer the following day. That's how faith works.

Visualize: Like many areas of life, visualization makes generosity *easier* and more *effective*. When you learn to see yourself, in your own mind being generous, it is much easier to do it in the physical.

Practice seeing yourself giving at church, to the guy ringing the bell outside the grocery store, or wherever else you encounter opportunities to be generous. Don't forget to visualize yourself giving more than just money. See yourself giving of your time, talent, information, ability, etc.

Don't Expect Anything: As I have discovered, you will get many returns on your generosity; just don't *expect* it! When you are expecting to be repaid for you kindness, you are doing it with the wrong motives.

Remember that you are in control of your actions, not the results. You could do good, but it might not be perceived that way by the recipient of your good deed or action. Should you stop doing good? Of course not.

Another thing to consider is that many times the good you receive from your generosity will come from *unexpected* places. If you are being generous, let it return to you. We will discuss this in the next section, but for now, stop keeping score!

Don't Forget To Accept Generosity

This often is an overlooked aspect of generosity. If you live life with a spirit of generosity, then you have the *right* and *obligation* to accept generosity from others.

Don't forget to accept generosity from others. Many times, people who have learned to give have a difficult time with allowing others to do nice things for *them*. It is perfectly ok to accept someone else's generosity, as long as you continue to do good for other people. In fact, it is an obligation, because by accepting someone else's generosity you are helping them to develop this critical trait.

True success is generous! In our culture today, we are constantly told about the *"secrets of success."* In fact, some people who are motivated by greed sell this illusion to unsuspecting people who are simply looking for a better life. In reality though, there are no *"secrets."* The ability for anyone to be successful exists, as long as they are following in their life purpose.

Don't Forget To Ask For Help

If you need help in pursuing the mission *you* have been called to on this earth, find someone who is successfully following a similar path. Ask them for help and guidance. They have *probably* encountered the difficulties that you are experiencing right now. They may have overcome those difficulties through years of trial and error. This could save you considerable time and trouble.

Truly successful people will be more than happy to assist you; to share with you what works and what doesn't. They are more than willing to mentor you and show you how to get through the difficulties. I'm not talking about the fool, who is out there, telling everyone how to do everything. I mean the quiet success, who is glad to help when asked.

If you ask someone for guidance and they refuse, then it's very likely that they are not as successful as they appear to be on the surface. Our world is *full* of people who have put on a good show to impress others. So, if this happens, consider yourself lucky; you have saved yourself a headache. Now, go and seek someone who is a **true success** to help you.

When you achieve success in your life, you have the same *responsibility* to give back and help others. When you do achieve it, make sure you remain generous about it. You can become the quiet success who is glad to help when asked.

It's time to begin accepting good things in your life.

See Action Step #10.

How To Bring Out The Best In Others

As every successful person understands, achieving one's own objective is simply not enough. Sooner or later, you realize that there is more to life than *just* achieving your own objectives. One of life's greatest challenges and most rewarding responsibilities is to continually encourage *others* to live up to their potential! Regardless of if you are a business leader, friend, parent or spouse, one of the most important obligations you have is to lift others to new levels of success and help them live to their potential. If done properly, this can be made into a winning situation for *all* involved.

It's important to realize that you are *always* influencing the people around you, in general and the people who look to you for leadership, in particular, either positively or negatively. Everything you say has an effect and your actions have significance. These words and actions can be used to build others up or tear them down. Obviously, you would prefer to build people up, I hope. Here are ten things *you* can do to help others identify and realize the best that's within them:

1.   **Believe In Them:** *Everyone* lacks confidence at times. Sometimes we question our abilities to achieve an objective or accomplish a task. Many times, that lack of confidence can be overcome just by knowing that someone believes in you. Having someone believe in you, in these circumstances, is immeasurable and is often the only thing that stands between failure and success. Think back to a time when someone believed in you, even when you doubted yourself. It made you feel good, didn't it? History is full of examples of great people who became successful because someone believed in them, even though they struggled with their own confidence.

2.   **Expect More:** I expect more from myself than *anyone* could ever ask of me; and I can guess that if you are following this program, that it is very likely that you do too. Unfortunately, many people around you have been conditioned by society, "not to get their hopes up." It's been my experience that the more you ask of someone, the more you will get. By increasing your expectations, you can lift other people up to new levels of achievement. Has there ever been a time when your boss handed you an

"impossible" project, expecting you to complete it and somehow you did? Be careful not to overwhelm someone, but do expect a lot.

3.   **Lead By Example:** One of the most effective ways to bring out the best in others is through your own actions. The way you *act*, both publicly and privately, says much more about you than what comes out of your mouth. Your kids are constantly watching you, for the way you react to *all* of life's circumstances and situations. You may tell your kids to eat their broccoli, but if you don't set the example by actually doing it yourself, they may do it to avoid being punished, but as soon as your gone, the broccoli's going to go straight into the trash. We naturally try to act like our mentors and you are a mentor to *someone*, so mentor by example!

4.   **Be A Source Of Encouragement:** How often do you encourage other people? With the pace of society today, it is very easy to get "caught up" in your day-to-day busyness and forget that you *can* really help someone by speaking words such as: "You can do it" or "I know you can." *Genuine* encouragement can go far in helping someone persevere. Making this a habit will lift everyone you come into contact with to new levels of success. Try saying to a friend, who may be having problems at home, "I know that you are going through a difficult time with your spouse, but I know that you two will work it out. Your relationship will come out even stronger in the end."

5.   **Always Tell The Truth:** Many people will avoid telling the truth, because they don't want to hurt someone's feelings or lose a friend. But in order to truly help someone, you must tell the truth! I know that you want to be liked, but telling the truth is an action that shows *real* concern and friendship. It may be, that what needs to be said, can only come from you. You're boyfriend or girlfriend drinks too much? By telling them and confronting the problem, you may not only help them stop, you may also let them realize how much you care.

6. **Expose Your Failures:** Your failures are the greatest learning experiences for *others* who may be doing what you tried to do in the past. Many people, to avoid looking vulnerable, will hide the failures that they have encountered. Showing other people that you have failed can really help them by showing them that everyone fails! In fact, the most successful people are the ones who have

failed the most. Be proud of your failures! You can use them to encourage other people and to remember where you have been. Telling your spouse about the broken dream you had, may be enough to keep her motivated in pursuing her vision.

7. **Praise Them**: Catch someone doing something *right*. It's easy to criticize others when they are not living up to your expectations. Over time, this leads to a breakdown of someone's self-esteem and their ability to encourage themselves. Learn to give positive feedback and you'll be amazed at the results. In my family, there is a rule that everyone must follow: every time you need to criticize someone, you must also give them ten compliments. If you are a sales manager, try this with someone on your team. When people know that they will get rewarded for positive actions, they tend to do them more often.

8. **Listen And Ask Good Questions:** A successful person doesn't tell other people what to do. They learn to *ask* thought-provoking questions, in order for others to rationalize decisions more clearly. This helps them to get clear on the implications of their choices. When the questions are asked, sit back and listen. Use why and how questions, as opposed to yes and no know questions; this will help them to make good choices, because they will come to their *own* conclusions. They will also learn to respect you as someone who they can trust. By asking well thought out questions, you cause others to think of their own solutions to problems, which will lead to more self-reliance.

9. **Learn To Motivate Others:** Learn what causes people in your life to be motivated. Everyone has *different* motivations and people who are "unmotivated" will only work hard enough to keep their current position in life. Someone who is sufficiently motivated will strive for excellence, in spite of the obstacles. Everyone needs to be challenged from time to time. This is how we grow and become better. Learning to challenge and motivate others is a skill that will not only improve your relationships, but also improve *everyone* around you. Think of someone you know that is just going through the motions of daily living; how can you motivate them?

10. **Invest Your Most Precious Asset:** Do you want to know what someone cherishes and respects? Watch to see where they spend their *time*. If you learn to invest your time in

people that you want to succeed, they will! You will communicate the message that they are important and they will learn to respect and value the time you spend with them. My seven-year-old son and four-year-old daughter know that I will drop everything and focus completely on them; they know that they're important and how much I love them. I have no doubt about their future success. Cancel your "night out" and spend time with those who *truly* matter. Use this most treasured of resources to lift others up! Remember, once your out of time, you can't do any more to help others.

Learning how to bring out the best in others is one of the most important skills you can learn. When you understand how to do this effectively, then you have truly become successful.

See Action Step #11.

Giving Back For The Gift You Have Found In This Program

The question you are *probably* asking yourself: "Why should I share this program with other people?" The answer is quite simple. Every time you share this program with another person, you are taking a step to *assure* that you don't slip back into your old lifestyle.

Sharing this program is a great way to repay others and society, in general, for your past misdeeds and mistakes. No, you can't change the past, but by introducing someone to this program, you are conveying the message that you care and that means a lot.

Sharing this program is fun, exciting, and fulfilling. Who knows, you may be altering someone's life *forever* in a positive way, just by telling him or her about us. Besides, what better way to spend the rest of your life, than by showing people a *better* way to live? Wouldn't it be great if you could *surround* yourself with people who are practicing this program?

Don't forget, that if this program has changed your life, then you have a moral and ethical obligation to let those who are closest to you share in the fruits of success. It is a completely selfless act, which is the very nature of this program and this principle.

Decide now what from this program you want to share. In this program, you have found love, acceptance, peace, freedom and success. Wouldn't it be nice to share *all* of these benefits with the world? I think so. Besides, you are *always* sharing this program in what you say and do. You are also sharing it in what you don't say and don't do.

See Action Step #12.

Conclusion

As it has been said, in The Babylonian Talmud: "I took the portion that was given me and gave it to him"[80]

Begin your journey of generosity today. You will be unlocking doors to your future that were never possible to go through before. You will be a blessing to everyone around you and in the process you will begin to make the world a better place for everyone, even you. That is an objective that we should all strive for. So go now and give. Give of your time, talent, money and anything else you can think of.

Summary

- Takers
- Keepers
- Givers
- Taking It One Step Further
- You Can Make a Difference
- You Will Harvest What You Plant.
- Tithing
- Generosity Above Tithing
- Being Generous Without Spending A lot Of Money
- How To Start Being Generous
  - Be Neighborly
  - Do Something Nice Everyday
  - Experiment
  - Share Information
  - Sow Encouragement
  - Offer Wisdom
  - Stand In Faith
  - Visualize
  - Don't Expect Anything
- Don't Forget To Accept Generosity
- How To Bring Out The Best In Others
  - Believe In Them
  - Expect More
  - Lead By Example
  - Be A Source Of Encouragement
  - Always Tell The Truth
  - Expose Your Failures
  - Praise Them
  - Listen And Ask Good Questions
  - Learn To Motivate Others
  - Invest Your Most Precious Asset
- Giving Back For The Gift You Have Found In This Program

Prayer for Generosity

God, help to guide me in my generosity. Let me be a giver of all the good you allow to flow in my life. Show me how to be generous in all that I do and to gracefully accept generosity from others. Amen.

Action Steps for Generosity

Generosity Action Step 1 – Being Generous To You

For now, do something nice for yourself; something you may not have thought you deserved. It doesn't have to be big or extravagant, just something to show yourself that you have value. Answer the following questions:

1.   What have you decided to do for yourself?

_____

_____

_____

2.   When do you plan on doing this?

_____

_____

_____

3.   After you follow through on activities 1 & 2 above, did you enjoy doing something nice for yourself? Why?

_____

_____

_____

4.   What are your thoughts, ideas and feelings about doing nice things for yourself?

_____

_____

_____

Generosity Action Step 2 – First Step Towards Generosity

For this Action Step, give something away. It can be anything that has value to you. You can give away your time by volunteering. You can give away some clothing to an organization that helps the needy. You can give away some money. The choice is yours. Once you have followed through on this, answer the following questions.

1. Who was helped by your generosity?

_____

_____

_____

2. How do you feel about it?

_____

_____

_____

3. What else can you give so that the flowing power of generosity works in your life?

_____

_____

_____

4. What are your thoughts, ideas and feelings about your first steps towards generosity?

_____

_____

_____

Generosity Action Step 3 – Takers, Keepers, Givers

For this Action Step examine your past and decide if you have been a taker, keeper or giver. Do the following exercises:

1. Are you a taker, keeper or giver?

   _____

   _____

   _____

2. How do you know?

   _____

   _____

   _____

3. Ask someone you know these questions about you. What did they say?

   _____

   _____

   _____

4. How would your life improve if you learned to be more generous?

   _____

   _____

   _____

5. What are your thoughts, ideas and feelings about takers, keepers and givers?

   _____

   _____

   _____

Generosity Action Step 4 – The Need For God

It's time to review the 5 main reasons that most people don't share God and see what's holding you back. Answer the following questions and do the activities.

1.   Are you concerned about other people? Are you willing to help someone who may hurt you? Prove it! Do something to help another person that you never thought you would. What will you do?

_____

_____

_____

2.   Are you knowledgeable about God? Are you willing to take the chance? Learn something new about God by reading your Bible or going to church. When will you do this?

_____

_____

_____

3.   Are you courageous in your mission to share God? Are you willing to be brave? Talk to someone about God who may reject, ridicule or criticize you. Who are you going to talk to? When?

_____

_____

_____

4.   Are you acting in faith? Are you willing to stand in faith? Do something today that is "impossible." What will you do?

_____

_____

_____

5.   Are you focused? Are you willing to focus on God's plan for your life? Develop a plan about how, where, why and when you will share God with other people. What is your plan?

_____

_____

_____

_____

_____

_____

_____

_____

_____

_____

_____

_____

_____

_____

_____

_____

_____

_____

_____

Generosity Action Step 5 – Sowing & Reaping

In this Action Step, you are going to begin the process of sowing good in your life. Do each of the activities listed below.

1.   List 5 things or results that you would like to reap in your life.

_____

_____

_____

2.   For each of the things or results listed in Step 1, list one activity you can sow into someone else's life.

_____

_____

_____

_____

_____

_____

_____

3.   Do each activity listed in step 2.

4.   What are your thoughts, ideas and feelings about sowing and reaping?

_____

_____

_____

_____

_____

Generosity Action Step 6 – Creative Generosity

In this Action Step, you are going to begin being generous with your money and other areas of your life. Think of what you can share with others, above and beyond just money. Start by answering these questions:

1. How much money can you comfortably give right now?

   _____

   _____

   _____

2. What person or organization should you give this money to?

   _____

   _____

3. What are some other creative ways that you can be generous?

   _____

   _____

   _____

4. What person or organization should you show this generosity towards?

   _____

   _____

   _____

5. What are your thoughts, ideas and feelings about creative generosity?

   _____

   _____

   _____

Generosity Action Step 7 – Start Being Generous

In this Action Step, there are two parts to complete. Doing these exercises will help to develop a generous attitude. Do the following:

Part 1:

1.	Make a list of all the things you can do for a neighbor. Do this even if you don't know them, don't like them or haven't spoken to them in years.

_____

_____

_____

_____

_____

2.	Decide which item from the previous questions you can do today.

_____

_____

_____

_____

_____

3.	Do it right now.

Generosity Action Step 7 – Part 2 –Start Being Generous

1.   Make a list of all the small things you can do for someone you don't even know.

_____

_____

_____

2.   Decide which item from the previous question you can do today.

_____

_____

_____

3.   Do it right now.

4.   What are your thoughts, ideas and feelings about starting to be generous?

_____

_____

_____

_____

_____

_____

_____

_____

_____

Generosity Action Step 8 ~ Experiment

In this Action Step, you are going to discover your unique abilities, talents and gifts that can be sown into the lives of other people.

1.   Make a list of your talents and gifts.

_____

_____

_____

2.   Do some research to figure out where these would be most useful. What did you discover?

_____

_____

_____

3.   Call an organization that may benefit from your talents and gifting. Offer to volunteer. When will you start?

_____

_____

_____

4.   What are your thoughts, ideas and feelings about your unique abilities, talents and gifts of generosity?

_____

_____

_____

_____

_____

_____

Generosity Action Step 9 – Sow Encouragement

In this Action Step, you will begin to develop a spirit of encouragement. Being a source of encouragement for others is a type of generosity that has many positive benefits. Sow encouragement into someone's life.

1.   List 3 people who you know need encouragement.

_____   _____   _____

2.   Write down something nice you can say to someone who needs encouragement today.

_____

_____

_____

3.   Send an email, letter, or just say something that encourages each of these people.

4.   What are your thoughts, ideas and feelings about sowing encouragement into other people's lives?

_____

_____

_____

_____

_____

_____

_____

_____

_____

Generosity Action Step 10 – Accepting Generosity & Help

In this Action Step, you will begin teaching yourself to accept generosity and ask for help from others.

Part A:

1.   List all of the times, in the past week, that people have offered you something nice and you refused.

_____

_____

_____

2.   If there are more than 5, pick the 3 biggest. For each of these 3, write down why you refused it.

_____

_____

_____

_____

_____

3.   Next, write down why you will accept generosity from others in the future.

_____

_____

_____

4.   Make a promise to yourself, that when you are offered generosity from other people, you will accept it.

_____

_____

_____

Generosity Action Step 10 – Part 2 – Accepting Generosity & Help

1. List all of the times in the past week that you needed help.

   _____
   _____
   _____

2. For each of the above, did you ask for help?

   _____
   _____
   _____

3. When you asked, did you receive help? Why or why not?

   _____
   _____
   _____

4. What are your thoughts, ideas and feelings about accepting generosity and asking for help?

   _____
   _____
   _____
   _____
   _____
   _____
   _____
   _____
   _____
   _____

Generosity Action Step 11 – How To Bring Out The Best In Others

In this Action Step, you will begin learning how to bring out the best in others. To complete these activities, review the section titled "How To Bring Out The Best In Others," starting on page 142

1.	Review the ten suggestions in this section. Which of these are you good at?

_____

_____

_____

2.	Which of these do you need to work on?

_____

_____

3.	Who is one person you can apply these suggestions towards to bring out the best in them?

_____

_____

_____

4.	What can you do right now for the person identified in question 3?

_____

_____

_____

5.	What are your thoughts, ideas and feelings about bringing out the best in others?

_____

_____

Generosity Action Step 12 - Introduce this program to one person today.

In this Action Step, you will begin practicing generosity by sharing this program with other people. To do this, complete the following activities.

1.   List 3 people who can benefit from this program:

_____   _____   _____

2.   Pick the person from the previous question, who needs this program, the most?

_____

_____

_____

3.   Give them our phone number, send them a link to our website or give them an "I Care Card" (found in the back of this book and on our website). Simply talk to them about us. You will be helping them, yourself, and us.

4.   Wouldn't it be beneficial if you did the same thing for the other 2 people on your list?

_____

_____

_____

5.   What are your thoughts, ideas and feelings about introducing this program to other people?

_____

_____

_____

I Care Cards

Hi _____,

I have found this new program, created by Family Coaching Central.

They have a system, consisting of lifetime fundamentals, to create real and lasting success. It is a very simple program that leads to fulfillment in life. I am excited about the changes that have been occurring in my life since beginning this program.

I am sending you this information because I care about you and know that this program will help you in so many ways.

You can learn more about this new, dynamic program at www.lifetimefundamentals.com. I hope you take a look at what they offer.

I am so excited!

_____

I Care Cards

Hi _____,

I have found this new program, created by Family Coaching Central.

They have a system, consisting of lifetime fundamentals, to create real and lasting success. It is a very simple program that leads to fulfillment in life. I am excited about the changes that have been occurring in my life since beginning this program.

I am sending you this information because I care about you and know that this program will help you in so many ways.

You can learn more about this new, dynamic program at www.lifetimefundamentals.com. I hope you take a look at what they offer.

I am so excited!

_____

I Care Cards

Hi _____,

I have found this new program, created by Family Coaching Central.

They have a system, consisting of lifetime fundamentals, to create real and lasting success. It is a very simple program that leads to fulfillment in life. I am excited about the changes that have been occurring in my life since beginning this program.

I am sending you this information because I care about you and know that this program will help you in so many ways.

You can learn more about this new, dynamic program at www.lifetimefundamentals.com. I hope you take a look at what they offer.

I am so excited!

_____

I Care Cards

Hi _____,

I have found this new program, created by Family Coaching Central.

They have a system, consisting of lifetime fundamentals, to create real and lasting success. It is a very simple program that leads to fulfillment in life. I am excited about the changes that have been occurring in my life since beginning this program.

I am sending you this information because I care about you and know that this program will help you in so many ways.

You can learn more about this new, dynamic program at www.lifetimefundamentals.com. I hope you take a look at what they offer.

I am so excited!

_____

The Principle of Health

Life is not merely to be alive but to be well
– Marcus Valerius Martial

Dear friend, I pray that you may enjoy good health and
that all may go well with you, even as your soul is
getting along well. 3 John 1:2 (NIV)

Take Care of you

It is your responsibility to take care of your health. No one else is going to do it; so don't expect them to. Whether you just ran the Boston Marathon and only need a gentle reminder or you haven't moved off the couch or eaten a green bean in years, let's go through this principle together. When my wife and I were in the planning stages of this program, I struggled with including a section on physical health. There are many people out there who ignore health and instead, are focusing on so many less important things. Just taking a look at the state of many people today would tell you that we, as a society, do not place enough importance on health and physical well-being. I finally decided to include this principle because I believe that the state of your overall self is absolutely depended on your physical health.

Your physical health tells a great deal about you. If you are unhealthy and out of shape, you will not have the strength, energy, stamina or even the confidence to do all that is necessary to make your life what it is meant to be. If you are not taking care of yourself, then at some level, you probably do not think very highly of yourself. If this is the case, just continue practicing the principles in this program and you will be able to have positive changes in all areas of your life, including your health.

See Action Step #1

The Truth About Health

For now, let's look at some possibly hard truths. It is very unlikely that if you are not taking care of your own physical health, that you are able to care for or help other people. It is probably about time you put down the Big Mac and milkshake, bought yourself a nice pair of running or hiking shoes and just realize what you may be missing out on by ignoring your health for so long.

It is possible that you have grown to hate or reject physical exercise or the planning necessary to eat a proper diet. If you allow it to be, it can be fun! You have simply been programmed into believing that it was something you *must* do, rather than believing that it is something that you *choose* to do. Beginning an exercise program and beginning to follow a healthy diet will help change all of your attitudes about healthy living and it will make you better able to start living your own healthy lifestyle.

I am talking about *simple* changes you can make to improve your quality of life. I would just like to caution you, if you haven't been paying attention, that the health industry is loaded with scams. Just know that you can't have "great abs" by just working out for 3 minutes a day and there is no magic food that will melt away those extra pounds. Also, there are many well-intentioned experts. Remember what was said in other principles about experts; they complicate things. Some of the experts you may encounter in your quest for better health include:

1. **Doctors** – I am sure that the vast majority of doctors out there have good intentions; the truth is that most doctors don't have the foggiest idea about staying healthy. In medical school, they learn about sickness and disease, not about staying healthy.

2. **Personal Trainers** – Sometimes, when I am at the gym working out, I watch the people who are being "trained." Some of these trainers have their clients doing some pretty wacky things in the name of getting healthy and fit. I am not saying that all personal trainers do this; I am simply stating some of what I have observed. The truth is, there are many good ones; the further truth is, that you don't need them to get and stay healthy. What you *do* need is the desire; no personal trainer can give or teach you that.

3. **Nutritionists** – I have heard some pretty strong claims from this group of "professionals," many of which are false. All you need to do is look at the diet trends that come and go to get a sense of the nutrition industry. They are taking the simple and complicating it. Again, I am sure that many nutritionists are fine people, but you don't need them. By following this program, you will be taught a sensible way to eat that works! You will make *your* own decisions based on logic and *your* body.

4. **Pharmaceutical Companies** – Simply read the small print in an advertisement for just about any medication; the cure is usually worse than the existing problem if you take into account the side effects of many prescription drugs. Again, they are probably very nice people, but they know very little about health.

The point that I am trying to make is that you need to make your own decisions about your own health. You need to develop a sensible plan for exercising, eating and staying healthy and then *stick* to that plan. Since the dawn of time, fears associated with sickness as well as getting and staying healthy have plagued most people. Don't fall into that trap. Take care of yourself now and you will not become a victim of the modern "snake oil" salesmen. There are so many other benefits to becoming and staying healthy and I will cover them here, but as with everything else, it is up to *you* to act.

Two Forces That Work Together

There are two major forces that work together to shape your overall health and well-being. These forces, applied separately, will not have the same effect as when you get them both working in your life. They are the forces of diet *and* exercise. I will talk about each one individually later. For now, I need to stress the point that for optimum health, it is important to focus on both of these.

Diet and exercise rely on *synergy*, where the whole, in this case diet and exercise, is greater than the sum of the parts. This simply means that the effect of these two forces together, is greater than if each of them were undertaken separately.

I know many people, and I am sure you do to, who have tried to incorporate either one of these into their lives without the other. The usual result is frustration and eventual loss of motivation and momentum. People who exercise, without a proper diet or focus on nutrition, will simply find that they do not have the energy to continue with their exercise program. People, who try to diet without an exercise program, will find themselves frustrated and usually return to their old eating habits. In both cases, the inability to continue with the healthy lifestyle change is caused by not incorporating *both* diet and exercise simultaneously.

Combine these two together and you create a lifestyle that will help you get through your day and fuel your vision. These two things enhance your desire to get healthy. I believe that they feed off of each other. It's quite obvious that if you start to make wise decisions about your diet, it becomes easier to make wise decisions about exercise. It is also true in reverse; if you are making wise choices with regard to exercise, you will find it easier to make wise decisions that enhance your diet.

The Benefits of a Healthy Lifestyle

"If you grow a healthy tree, you'll pick healthy fruit. If you grow a diseased tree, you'll pick worm-eaten fruit. The fruit tells you about the tree."[81] These words can apply to many different areas of life. They are very true when applied to your health. You will get exactly what you put into your plan of health. There are so many benefits from living a healthy lifestyle that they are too numerous to mention. I will briefly touch on the main ones here:

1. **Increased Brain Function:** You will get smarter! It will be easier for you to solve problems and you will improve your memory significantly. This will make you more productive and increase your mental focus. Your concentration will improve too.

2. **Improved Relationships:** Whether you go for a walk with your spouse, or practice soccer with you children, you will be spending *more* time with them. Planning meals and cooking also becomes an activity you can do together.

3. **Less Stress:** Life can be stressful. Proper diet and physical movement help reduce stress. You will be more relaxed in all areas of your life. Your mood will improve and you will avoid depression, which will help you in every area of this program.

4. **More Energy:** When you are healthy it is much easier to accomplish everyday tasks like cleaning the house or cutting the grass. It also allows you to do tasks that may not be routine. You will have energy to work on your *whole* life. You will be energized throughout your day. You may feel more tired at first, but that will go away as you continue to work on your health.

5. **Increased Strength and Endurance:** *Everything* you do will get easier! This will help with all activities from climbing the stairs, to opening a jar of pickles.

6. **Increased Self-Esteem:** Learning to get your health under control will have an amazing effect on the way you feel about *yourself*. It's just a simple truth that when you look better, you feel better.

7. **Increased Self-Discipline:** Finding the time to exercise and following through when you don't really want to, as

well as taking the time to eat better will transfer to every area of your life. This will help you with the self-discipline needed to follow through on the rest of these principles.

8. **Better Sleep:** Your sleep will be much more rewarding. This will help to keep you refreshed and better able to live the rest of your life in a successful and fulfilling manner.

9. **Less Disease and Illness**: A healthy lifestyle makes your immune system stronger. It also helps to fight off many of the common diseases that people experience as they age. When you do experience an illness, you will recover faster.

10. **Improved Sex Life:** It is clear to see that if you experience the preceding nine benefits, then this area of your life will improve too.

I hope that I have convinced you of the importance of adopting a healthy lifestyle and that you should begin *now* eating right and exercising everyday. Just in case I haven't, I am including the following list of benefits (hopefully something will get your attention):

- Weight Loss
- Better Complexion
- Better Digestion
- Improved Flexibility
- Lower Blood Pressure
- Better Appetite
- Better Agility
- Improved Posture
- Reduced Injury
- Slows Aging
- Prevents Stroke
- Prevents Diabetes
- Prevents Osteoporosis
- Improved Cardiovascular Function

- Lower Resting Heart Rate
- More Motivation
- Improved Athletic Performance
- Improved Concentration
- Improved Nervous System
- Improved Body Shape
- Improved Body Image
- Improved Muscular Definition
- Improved Circulation
- Increased Lean Muscle Mass
- Eases Menstrual Pain
- Better Balance
- Eliminates Back Pain
- Improved Liver Function
- Prevents Heart Disease
- Lowers Cholesterol
- Prevents Arthritis
- Strengthens Heart
- Lower Breast Cancer Risk
- More Efficient Metabolism
- Less Joint Pain
- Increased Life Span
- Improved Reaction Time
- Eliminates Varicose Veins

Are you convinced yet? I could go on indefinitely listing all the benefits, but the truth is that a solid plan of exercise, diet and health has a positive impact on *every* area of your life. At the same time, neglecting these things in your life, has a negative impact on *every* area of your life. Most people already know the benefits of living a healthy lifestyle; I am sure that you weren't too shocked by the list of benefits. Stop struggling and start making this type of lifestyle a reality.

How? By following some simple instructions and guidance. If you already have a plan in place, then this principle may help to give you some new, fresh ideas that will help to keep you moving forward in this area of your life. If you learn one new idea, it will be worth it. I hope that "you may enjoy good health and all may go well with you, even as your soul is getting along well."[82]

See Action Step #2

Physical Activity

Plato definitely had it right when he said that, "lack of activity destroys the good condition of every human being, while movement and methodical physical exercise save and preserve it."[83]

Physical activity is just what it implies...MOVE! Move often! We live in a world where it is easy to avoid too much physical activity, if that is what you choose to do. If it weren't for the occasional broken elevator, few people would ever take the stairs. If it weren't for the fact that the TV and the refrigerator were so far apart, then many people would never get off the couch. Our bodies were made for movement. Many people don't understand that the simple reason they are always feeling tired is because they just don't get enough activity. If they would only get their body moving, they would feel better instantly. I will discuss physical activity as it relates to three areas of life. Those areas are exercise, general movement and play. They are all important and they all serve a purpose.

Types of Physical Exercise

Exercise is of extreme importance to a well-rounded, successful life. It has been said, "Those who think they have not time for bodily exercise will sooner or later have to find time for illness."[84]

When it comes to exercise, you do not need expert or expensive training to begin. Just start *somewhere*. I choose to go to the gym for most of my workouts, because of the variety of equipment and machines, but you don't have to, *especially* if you are just beginning. Of all movement you need to do on a daily basis, organized exercise is probably the easiest to ignore. I, however, believe it is probably the most important.

Our bodies were created for *movement*. In today's society there isn't much opportunity to do what our bodies were meant to do. Today, we have drive-through everything, remote controls and a culture that says that it is ok to be a couch potato. It's no wonder that so many in our society are out of shape and paying the price for it.

The only way to combat this trend is to get regular exercise. God did not design our bodies to be sitting behind a desk, at a computer, for 12 hours a day. If you don't believe me on this, take a 30-day challenge. For the next 30 days, get some exercise at least 3 to 4 days a week. The exercise should consist of cardio, strength, flexibility and agility training.

You will be amazed at the results. You will have more energy and stamina; you will be more confident in everything you do and you will be more efficient. Believe it or not, the 90 minutes you *"waste"* in the gym will translate into more productive time so that you will get more done. You will also be happier with yourself and the world around you. Try it!

I have found that *all* four of the types of exercise mentioned above are important and they all serve a purpose. **Cardio training** is used to get your cardiovascular system working more efficiently. This type of training will help you to not get winded when having to do other tasks. You will also develop endurance by doing cardio training. Some examples of cardio training include running (or walking if you're just getting started), biking or taking a cardio kick boxing class.

Strength training is important to help build your muscles. Building muscle mass is of far more importance than just trying to look good at the beach from June through August. Strength training will help you accomplish everyday tasks in a more efficient manner. Whether you struggle with opening a pickle jar or carrying the groceries in from the car, you will benefit from including this type of exercise in to your routine. Some examples of strength training include working out with weights and machines, or just doing exercises with your own body weight, such as push-ups and pull-ups. Strength training should also include work on your core, such as crunches and leg lifts.

The next two categories of exercise are the *most* neglected. Even among people who claim to be healthy or are otherwise in good shape, these two are often overlooked. Most people completely miss out on the benefits of flexibility and agility training.

Flexibility training is designed to help you move easier. Stretching increases your body's flexibility and range of motion. The benefits of doing this type of training can be seen everywhere. From being able to easily bend over to tie your shoes to being able to stretch just a little bit more to change a blown out light bulb, your whole body will benefit from a stretching routine. I guarantee that your *entire* body will feel better when you begin to stretch, even if you have been exercising for years. You should be stretching *all* of your muscle groups. To find instructions for your flexibility training, simply do an Internet search; you will find all the information you need to get started.

Agility training is necessary so that you learn to move more efficiently. This last type of exercise that you should be doing is by no means the least important. In fact, you probably won't have much success with agility training, unless you are able to work on the other areas, but doing agility conditioning will help you to move better and to enjoy life a whole lot more. I like to call agility training, functional strength. You will gain the ability to move in a significant way by completing this form of exercise on a regular basis. I do Martial Arts training to gain and increase my agility, but there are many other activities that you can participate in to help you in this area. Agility training will also help you develop balance and other body control. This will translate into more efficient movement in your everyday life.

See Action Step #3

You need to find the combination of these different types of exercises that work best for you. It all depends on what your needs are. Also, don't forget that your needs will change as your lifestyle changes. I remember when my son Michael and I started taking karate together. My flexibility wasn't nearly where it should have been (because of years of neglect); so I focused on that area everyday. Once the desired level of flexibility was achieved, it no longer had to be done as much. It still needs to be done, but not as much, so other areas of exercise can be given more attention. Here are some tips to help you maintain your program:

- **Don't worry about *occasionally* missing workouts.** I know many people who have gotten so angry with themselves for missing workouts. They allowed this anger to build to the point where they associated a great deal of pain with exercise; they no longer exercise.

- **Don't get so serious about your exercise program, that it is no longer fun.** This is the surest way to guarantee your failure. Keep it fun and you will continue with it for years, even after many of the other people around you quit or slip out of their own program.

- **There are no shortcuts.** To reap the benefits, you have to do the work. Don't be fooled into thinking there is a "faster " way to exercise, or that you can get as healthy doing "five-minute abs," two times a week, as someone who is in the gym everyday sweating and working out.

Like most things in life, there are extremes when it comes to exercise. Some people focus on all other areas of spirituality, neglecting exercise because they don't see the connection of the two, or they don't think it's important. Other people take exercise and turn it into an all-consuming activity. They neglect other areas of spirituality and focus on exercise (which by itself has nothing to do with spirituality). Neither of these extremes indicates a balance in life. "For physical training is of some value, but godliness has value for all things, holding promise for both the present life and the life to come."[85] Exercise, when combined with a spiritual program of success, has an immense value; just don't overdo it!

Movement

It seems silly to be discussing general movement, as a way to maintain health, but it really is not. Some of us have become so accustomed to minimizing our movement on a daily basis that when we finally embrace a program like this, where physical activity is encouraged, it may take some time to get used to. In this program I am not talking about the movement necessary to switch the TV channel or the finger movement needed to win that video game. No, I am talking about consistent movement to accomplish daily tasks. I am talking about not always doing what seems easy and convenient, but rather seeking opportunities to move our body, even when society is telling us we shouldn't. There are almost *unlimited* possibilities to increase your daily movement. The best way to accomplish this is to stop looking for the easy way out. Take the stairs instead of going on the elevator; go into the bank instead of using the drive-thru. These may not seem very important and by themselves they really aren't. It's when all of these opportunities to move are strung together into a lifestyle pattern that they make a big difference. "Movement is a medicine for creating change in a person's physical, emotional, and mental states."[86] So move often!

Play

Movement is a *key* ingredient to success and happiness. Many people in society today have forgotten how good it feels to move in a significant way. I'm not talking about the movement required to roll off the couch in search of a lost remote control. I'm talking about the type of movement that makes life enjoyable and meaningful. I'm talking about turning the TV off, shutting down the computer and getting outside to enjoy everything and everyone around you.

Several years ago, my wife and I were drawn into a game of tag with our nieces and nephew, who ranged in ages from 8 to 12 years old. The game started off slowly, but soon picked up in intensity. Before long, I was running at full speed; having more fun than I had experienced in quite some time. The game lasted for several hours and we were all finally exhausted. That's when it hit me: I just got finished with the best exercise session I have had since I was a kid. I didn't even realize it either, at the time. I used muscles that I hadn't used in years and probably never could working out in a gym. That's when I became a believer of using play to exercise.

I am a big proponent of organized exercise. I believe that it helps to keep me growing in every area of my life. Organized exercise helps with your confidence, discipline, energy, spiritual growth and obviously your overall health. I think that everyone should have a structured exercise program, that keeps them committed and focused on achieving optimum performance and health; but now, after this game of tag, I am convinced that exercise in the form of play is equally, if not more beneficial to the human spirit. I felt better physically than I have after running 4 miles and at the same time I strengthened bonds with family members that will last a lifetime.

I was sore for the next several days after our game and I also thought about the possibility of injury, which would hurt my overall exercise program. Then I realized that the benefits I received from our game of tag far *outweighed* any potential risks. I always look forward to my next opportunity to play and always enjoy a challenging game of dodge ball with my kids.

See Action Step #4

What Should My Diet Consist Of?

With all of the different choices in food, it is sometimes very difficult to make proper choices. Consistently making poor choices in this area of life is much more destructive to your overall health and well-being than you may have ever realized. We live in a marketing based society, naturally every company that sells food wants you to buy theirs. That is where many people run into problems. They look at the commercials, the ads on the billboards and the labels on the packaging. By their very nature, many of these are misleading and unfortunately, it encourages a lifestyle that promotes lack of energy and poor health. As I write this section I am thinking about all the times I have fell victim to the famous "Big Mac Attack." Maybe you have experienced this too. You are driving down the highway and come across a billboard for a fast food restaurant. You think nothing of it in the moment, but a short time later, you want something from a fast food restaurant.

There are also the labels you run across in the grocery stores, that make all kinds of claims, many of them false or only partially true. Later in the program I mention some of the examples. I don't need to mention them here again, but just be aware of them.

On top of all of this, if you do decide to pursue a healthy lifestyle, you have an almost unlimited number of diet programs. They all claim that they are the way to a lifetime of health. The problem is that many of these programs contradict each other.

The Way To Make Sense Of Your Food

Food is important! Obviously, we can't live without it but we also must remember that some of the stuff that passes for food today has no business being put into our bodies. We must develop a sustainable plan that will give us the nourishment and strength we need to make our lifestyles healthy. In this section of the program I will share with you what has helped me and what I believe is a smart and sensible way to provide your body with the fuel it needs. More important than what I say, is your responsibility to trust your body. Your body is an amazing creation. It *always* knows what it's own nutritional needs are. You just simply need to listen and give it what it wants.

The more you eat what's good for you, the better your body will get at communicating this to you. No, your body is not going to start using words. Your body communicates with you through cravings. That "Big Mac" attack you had last week, might have been your body telling you that it needed protein. That craving you had for a candy bar was probably your body telling you that it needed more fuel, which you could have provided in the way of much more beneficial carbohydrates. It is *your* job to figure out what your body is trying to tell you. You must "translate" your cravings into sensible choices, when possible. It may be that you just wanted some fast food or a candy bar and that's okay, if it is the *exception* rather than the rule.

See Action Step #5

Twelve Tips For Eating Right:

I have included twelve tips that I have made a part of my diet and everyday life. They have helped me considerably in how I feel each day. Take these tips and adapt them to your own lifestyle.

1. **Drink Lots Of Water:** Your body is made mostly of water. Doesn't it make sense that you need a lot of it? Stay hydrated by drinking water. Pour out the sugary drinks and replace them with water. Most of the stuff you're drinking doesn't actually quench your thirst and may make you even thirstier. Don't be fooled by the fancy "sports drinks" either. Many of these are nothing more than soda, without the bubbles. Water is cleansing, rejuvenating and energizing. To make sure you get enough water, take your body weight in pounds and divide it in half. That is the *minimum* number of ounces of water that you should have per day. For

example, if you weigh 180 pounds, you should drink at least 90 ounces of water per day.

2. **Fruits and Vegetables:** Most fruits and vegetables have a very high water content, many as high as 75-80%. It should make sense to have these nutrient, water rich foods as an important part of a successful eating regimen. I found, while creating my healthy diet, that it was very easy to eat fruit but it was more difficult to fit vegetables into my diet. But you need to eat both and together they should be at least 70 percent of your overall food intake.

I came across an alarming study that found most adults are eating fewer vegetables than ever, even if you count french fries.[87] Here are some ways you can make sure that you don't become another statistic. As always, if you find something useful, incorporate it into your plan:

- **Eat them raw.** This is the best way to get the maximum benefit. Also, it will save time. Many people skip vegetables simply because they don't have the time to cook them.

- **Look for prepackaged ones.** If you have tried and you just can't stand raw vegetables then find ones that have most of the prep work done. If they are already sliced, washed and chopped or peeled then it will take much less time to prepare them.

- **Spice them up.** Add herbs and spices to your vegetables to make them taste better.

- **Make them into something.** Try making a vegetable soup or a pasta sauce with a *variety* of chopped vegetables.

- **Hide them in other dishes.** Make an artichoke or spinach pizza. Put lettuce and tomatoes on your sandwich.

- **It's best to eat them raw and plain.** If you just can't do this, then add other things to them. Get creative. The important thing is to make sure you eat them *every day*!

- **Have a salad.** I try to have a salad with *every* meal. It allows for variety and cuts down on the boredom of eating the same things all the time. Try a fruit salad for breakfast and vegetables at lunch and/or dinner.

- **Have juice.** If *all* else fails, make them into a juice; hold your nose and gulp them down. I prefer to make juices that have fruits *and* vegetables. The sweetness of the fruits makes them more appetizing (using overly ripened pineapple or oranges adds to the sweetness). This isn't the best way to get your vegetables, but it's better than nothing.

3. **Protein:** If you plan on following through on any significant exercise program, and I hope I have convinced you of the necessity of doing so, then you will *need* protein in your diet. How much depends on how intense you are exercising and your individual needs. To understand the importance of protein, you must have a *basic* understanding of what happens when you exercise and what role protein plays. To keep it simple, you just need to understand that as you exercise, you are actually tearing your muscle fibers. Protein is used by your body to rebuild these fibers. Without it, you will rob your body of the food it needs to heal itself in order to get ready for the next exercise session. Types of protein include animal proteins such as meat, fish, chicken, eggs, milk and cheese. There are also plant-based proteins, such as beans, nuts and some vegetables. You will need to experiment with how much your body needs. The key is to listen to *your* body. Your body will tell you exactly what type and how much protein you need. After a short time, you will get good at listening. You will be able to judge by your workout, exactly what your body needs.

4. **Dark food:** I know that this is not the case with every single type of food, but a good rule to follow is always choose darker foods over lighter colored types of food. Most light colored or white food is processed. It is also important to know that dark food usually contains more vitamins and other nutrients that the body needs. Start to do your own research on this and you will find that what I am saying will help you in your pursuit of better health. The best research I have found is active

experimentation. See what foods work for you and notice the difference that you feel. For example, if you start to use dark honey to sweeten things instead of white sugar, you will begin to feel better almost immediately. Some other examples include using brown rice instead of white, dark fruit juices instead of light and whole grains instead of bleached white flour.

5. **Choose Food Over Caffeine:** Learn to recognize high-energy foods and use them to replace the coffee that you normally use to give yourself the energy boost you need. I know what you're thinking, and I struggle with this one too, but as with most "quick fixes" in life, there is a down side. By relying on caffeine or other drugs to get you through the day, you are putting stuff in your body that doesn't belong there. By relying on these substances, your body usually requires more and more of them to achieve the same effect which leads to dependence on them just to help you get through the day. Instead, try choosing high-energy foods that will give you the boost you need, while at the same time, giving your body some essential nutrients. Some good choices include beans (such as black or pinto). These beans supply your body with a source of low-calories and steady energy; nuts and seeds work good as well. If you want you can mix these into your own trail mix or learn to make homemade granola bars. Also, try citrus fruits for a quick energy boost. Try oranges, grapefruit or pineapples which are all great sources of vitamin C.

6. **Variety:** Add variety to your diet. It's easy to get frustrated when your kids eat macaroni and cheese every night, but you probably never looked at your own behavior. Have you been eating the same turkey sandwich every day for lunch? It's easy to get caught up in eating the same thing every day in our busy society. Besides, if you do that, then there is no thought required and less time figuring out what to eat. By eating the same thing day after day, you rob your body of crucial vitamins and minerals since there is no single food that satisfies every nutritional need.[88] If you've been eating plain cheese pizza everyday for 10 years, try chicken salad instead. You may be pleasantly surprised and in the process, you may even add a new dimension of enjoyment to your day.

7. **Regular Mealtimes:** I know that this is difficult for most people, but if you learn to eat at the same time *daily*, you will actually eat less. Your body will become more effective at signaling to your brain when you are hungry and when you are full. There will be times when it just isn't possible, but strive for this. Eating at the same time also allows you to avoid unscheduled snacking, which if done consistently, will derail any nutrition program. We all know that a well planned, healthy and nutritious snack can supply us with much needed energy to keep us going when we feel tired or low on energy. When the snacking is unplanned, there is confusion in the body about when you will be eating again; then it tends to be harmful. If you need a snack at a certain time of day, then plan it into your schedule. It is common knowledge that it is beneficial to have more meals with smaller portions. Schedule a *small* meal as your snack. Just make sure your snack contains ingredients that are beneficial for your body. Most unplanned snacks contain food that is only food in the loosest sense of the word. Also, use common sense. A recent study found that dieters ate more food in a sitting when they were supplied with "mini packs" of food, such as the 100-calorie packs, that are being marketed today. The small portion sizes make people feel as if they can worry less about going overboard.[89] Eat low fat, high protein snacks or choose fruits and vegetables. These choices will make you feel full until your next meal.

8. **Read Labels:** Don't be fooled by our misleading, marketing driven society. Read your food labels *carefully*. Read what's actually in your food and don't skip over the big words that are difficult to pronounce; those are the important ones; research them. Find out what they are and make your own decision about whether you want to put it into your body, based on your own research. You may be surprised when you dig a little beneath the surface. Many labels are designed to sell food, not to convey what's *actually* inside the package. You may look at a label that reads "100%* fruit juice," and think that you're getting the real thing, but if you follow the "*" down to the small print on the bottom or on the back label, you will see in tiny print, phrases like "with added ingredients." Read what those "added" ingredients are. You may pick up

a bottle of juice that calls itself raspberry/apple juice. It may have an overwhelming number of raspberries in the picture on the label and maybe one small apple off in the corner; read the ingredients because it is very likely that you are about to purchase something that actually contains mostly apple juice and very little raspberry juice (or has raspberry flavoring)!

9. **Avoid Processed Food:** I can make this really *simple*. Food that is ground, bleached, sent through machines or otherwise processed is not good for you, period. I know that many processed foods taste good and I catch myself getting fooled by their convenience. They are not good for you! These foods, in addition to what I mentioned above, are usually high in salt and fat. Ingredients such as high fructose corn syrup, which is getting a lot of bad press lately, is not good for you. Chickens don't have nuggets. The list could be endless; bottom line is if it is "made" in a factory, don't eat it. Eat all natural foods whenever possible. Use sense here too; don't eat things just because they are "all natural" either. You can take a walk in the forest and find many varieties of "all natural" poisonous mushrooms, but that doesn't mean you should eat them. The rule to use here is to think about what you're eating and ask yourself if it makes sense. If you have to think too long, then don't eat it.

10. **Eat When Hungry:** Overeating is a problem in our society today. The list of reasons for overeating is endless and a large segment of our society is overweight and even obese. Remember to eat only when you are hungry. Do not fall victim to the sin of gluttony.[90] Today, many people tend to use food to ease stress. In a society where everything is fast paced and pressure is intense, don't develop the habit of eating three bowls of ice cream at the end of the day as a comfort to help you relax. Instead, find some type of activity that helps you to relax or try just taking some quiet time. Don't eat just because everyone else is eating. We all want to "fit in," but if you eat because you're at a business meeting, holiday event or other type of party then you will be harming your regimen. Lastly, in spite of everything you were taught growing up, you do not have to eat *everything* on your plate. If you eat even when you're not hungry, you cross over from being in control to gluttony. If you

really don't want to waste the food on your plate and you shouldn't want to; wrap the food and put it in the refrigerator. You can have it tomorrow and you will save the time of having to prepare a meal. Make sure you stop eating when you feel full!

11. **Chew:** Learn to *enjoy* your food. If you just sit down and eat as fast as you can, hoping to get on to your next activity, you are missing out on a lot of enjoyment. Instead, slow down; learn to notice the different tastes and textures; to recognize the different spices. Chewing your food thoroughly also helps with digestion. Your body will absorb more of the nutrients and will work more efficiently and effectively while you are pursuing and working on the other principles in this program. Set your fork down between bites and chew your food at least 20 times.

12. **Give Thanks:** Sadly, we live in a world where many people go hungry every single day. You have food in front of you, so give thanks for it. Acknowledge God for blessing you with *His* provision! Don't feel guilty or ashamed about the blessing you have received in the form of being able to nourish your body; that is not the point. Just be thankful you have the blessing that God has given you! Even if you don't believe it, God supplied you with the food you ate today. Many people fail to realize this and they assume that *they* are responsible and that *they* created this blessing in their life. Remember, "When you have eaten and are satisfied, praise the Lord your God for the good land He has given you"[91]

The above guidelines are meant as general rules only. They are what worked for me and continue to work for me today. Of course, it is *your* responsibility to make sure that you take *your* health into *your* own hands. The tips I have just outlined will help keep you energized and vibrant as you work on the other Principles in this program. Don't expect to wake up tomorrow and suddenly be healthy and strong if it has been years since you exercised or ate anything that was actually healthy. Just stay on track and gradually, over time, your health will improve.

See Action Step #6

Other Things For Health

There are some other things that I have found to help improve your health. Some of these ideas may seem like common sense to you, some of them you may not have thought of. I throw them out to you now, as ideas you can use and work on, to help you in your pursuit of physical health.

The first one is to *avoid* drugs and alcohol. At their worst they cause broken families, broken lives and much pain. At their best they cause drowsiness and lack of ambition. "Who has woe? Who has sorrow? Who has strife? Who has complaints? Who has needless bruises? Who has bloodshot eyes? Those who linger over wine, who go to sample bowls of mixed wine. Do not gaze at wine when it is red, when it sparkles in the cup, when it goes down smoothly! In the end it bites like a snake and poisons like a viper. Your eyes will see strange sights and your mind imagine confusing things. You will be like one sleeping on the high seas, lying on top of the rigging. 'They hit me,' you will say, 'but I'm not hurt! They beat me, but I don't feel it! When will I wake up so I can find another drink?'"[92] My experience and work with other people has shown that you can insert any type of alcohol or drug in the above statement and you will end up with the same result. Also, don't be fooled by the so-called "legal" drugs (prescription and non-prescription). My best advice to you is this: avoid drugs and alcohol like the plague! They will kill your success and your dreams, or at the very least, they will make it much harder to be successful.

The next suggestion I have is to make sure you laugh hard and laugh often. Laugh with your family. Laugh with your friends. Laugh with co-workers. Laugh with enemies...yes, enemies, if you can. When I learn to laugh at my faults and mistakes, it makes it much easier to work through them. Laughing will improve your personality and your overall outlook on life. So go out and rent a funny movie or buy a joke book; just start laughing. Remember that it is okay to laugh at yourself. When other people are involved, make sure you aren't laughing at them, but *with* them. Laughter is contagious, if you begin laughing, you just might get other people laughing with you and by doing this, you just might make, not only your life, but also the lives of everyone around you a little bit better.

See Action Step #7

The next suggestion I have is to fast on a *regular* basis. It's okay; you can make it for a short period of time without food.

Start small and gradually increase the amount of time. Fasting cleans the built up toxins out of your body and allows your body to repair itself. The simple explanation for this is that if you deprive your body of food for a short time, it will begin looking for other sources of energy. Rather than attacking healthy tissue and cells in your systems, it will go after the "bad" stuff first. This includes unhealthy cells and bodily tissue, thereby eliminating this harmful stuff. Fasting for too long will cause your body to begin going after the healthy cells and bodily tissue. I generally try to fast for twenty-four hours once every two weeks. Sometimes however, I may fast for up to forty-eight hours every thirty days or so. If you are new to fasting, I suggest you try a twenty-four hour fast to begin with. As with everything else in this principle, *listen* to your body. It is an amazing creation and it knows exactly what it needs.

On top of the physical benefits of fasting, you have the added benefit of experiencing a great deal of spiritual and mental growth. You will clear your mind and feel "cleaner" in your spirit. You might have a problem that you have been working on before fasting and suddenly, during the fast; you are supplied with the answer. If the fast is combined with a definite amount of prayer, which I cover in another principle, you will feel an unexplainable and incredible closeness with God. I receive enormous benefits from combining the two, fasting and prayer. If you give it a try, you will see why this combination is much more effective and beneficial when the period of prayer takes place at the end of the fasting period. Experiment with this and see what works best for you. Keep a journal of how you feel physically, mentally and spiritually – before, during and after your fasts.

See Action Step #8

Breathing is another important factor that you shouldn't overlook. It sounds simple enough; you breathe all the time, right? However, effective breathing is so important and most don't utilize it to its full potential. When done properly, breathing gives you energy and cleanses your body, thereby improving your health. Whenever you consciously remember, take long, slow, deep breaths. Over time, you will train your body to breathe like that naturally. It is also important to follow a simple plan of breathing exercises. This will help to move the stored toxins through and out of your body. You will also get the added benefits of stress reduction and relaxation. The best and most effective exercises consist of breathing in the following pattern:[93]

1. Inhale for 1 count

2. Hold for 4 counts

3. Exhale for 2 counts

In other words, if you take a deep breath for 5 seconds, hold it for 20 seconds and exhale for 10 seconds, you are doing these exercises *correctly*. If the time is too long, or if you feel lightheaded, dizzy or sick when doing these exercises cut down on the length of time and do a shorter cycle. Remember to keep the same ratio though. You can try taking a deep breath for 2 seconds, holding it for 8 seconds and exhaling for 4 seconds. You can work up to the longer cycle as you get healthier. For optimum benefit, you should do 10 of these cycles at least 3 times a day.

See Action Step #9

Create A Plan

I thought about supplying sample exercise plans and sample diets in this principle, but I decided against it. At first, I thought that if I supplied the plans, then more people would follow through. As I thought about it further, I realized that if somebody were going to follow through, they would be willing to do the work. I believe that if it is important *enough* to you and I gave you the facts, you would do the research and figure out exactly what you need to do. I did not want to influence *your* health needs with what I do. You need to figure out what will work best for you.

Keep it simple and remember: "To insure good health: eat lightly, breathe deeply, live moderately, cultivate cheerfulness, and maintain an interest in life."[94] Find people who are getting the results you want and talk to them. If you want to lose weight, find someone who has already lost weight. If learning a martial art is an objective of yours; find someone who is a black belt. Talk to friends, family or coworkers but always make sure the advice you choose to use makes sense. As you continue to learn about your health, the plan may change, but start now to develop a plan that works. As you gain knowledge about keeping yourself physically healthy, you can develop a comprehensive plan. For now, I will keep it very basic to help you get started. If you are already experienced in the areas of diet and exercise, then this may be a great time for you to review what you are currently doing and make the necessary adjustments you have been avoiding.

For your exercise program, map out what types of exercise you will do for each day of the week. Remember to take 1 or 2 days off for yourself to recover. In Action Step #3, you started to formulate a plan for exercise success; turn back to that Action Step. Remember to balance your activity between strength, cardio, flexibility and agility training.

For your diet, figure out what types of food you will be eating. Start by examining Action Step #5, where you recorded what you ate over a 24-hour period. Figure out what has been harming you and what has been beneficial by reviewing the "Twelve Tips For Eating Right," starting on page 185. Do some research, if you have to. It will be well worth your time.

See Action Step #10

Stick To Your Plan

The purpose of this principle is to convey the importance of staying well. You will never grow spiritually if you are out of shape and overweight. I meet many people who are seeking a successful spiritual life but they often fall short. Many times, it is the lack of proper diet and physical activity that causes them to fall down. "Do you not know that your body is a temple of the Holy Spirit, who is in you, whom you have received from God? You are not your own; you were bought at a price. Therefore honor God with your body."[95] I often find that this is an overlooked missing link between a mediocre life and a great life.

The following suggestions will help you stick to a plan of health, even after the newness wears off:

1. **Involve Others.** Cooking healthy meals with your kids, or going to the gym with your spouse will allow you to spend quality time together. You will help to keep each other on course if one of you begins to falter. Involve as many people as possible; family, friends, co-workers or neighbors are all possible choices. Who knows, you may be helping them stick to a plan of health, as well.

2. **Take Action.** I can guarantee that there will be days when you just don't want to stick to your plan. On these days, just do what you can to stay on

track. Do some jumping jacks and then eat a salad. If that is too much, move your thumbs; just do *something*! Seriously, go for a walk with your daughter or instead of going to happy hour on Friday afternoon, take your family out to dinner. Get the salad bar.

3. **Think.** Use exercise times as opportunities to think. Get out and get some exercise; spend some time playing. Do it now! Put this program down for thirty minutes. It will still be here when you get done. You will feel better physically and will probably mentally digest some important information about the principles in this program. When you are exercising or playing your brain is still working. It doesn't work the other way though. Sit in a chair for thirty minutes thinking. See if your legs start moving. If they do, you probably need to see a doctor. Your mind is probably working better now that you have gotten some physical activity. Maybe you should try that everyday before you begin working.

4. **Avoid Vanity.** It's important to feel good about yourself when you begin a program of physical health. Your confidence will improve and you will look better. Don't allow this feeling of well-being to cross over from a benefit to a liability by becoming vain. Never think that you are better than someone else because you look better in the mirror. "...Do not think of yourself more highly than you ought, but rather think of yourself with sober judgment, in accordance with the measure of faith God has given you."[96] If you fall into vanity, you will quickly erase any gains you would have otherwise made from this principle. Don't avoid someone who is new to the Principle Of Physical Health simply because they are out of shape. Instead, help them along and be a power of example for them.

5. **Stay Positive.** A positive attitude will get you moving towards your health objectives, even when you are having a bad day. "A cheerful disposition is good for your health; gloom and doom leave you bone-tired."[97] I have found that when I am dealing with some negative feelings and I don't feel like working on health, it's best to just get moving. Get

started on something. Whether it's planning the menu or working out, *momentum* has a way of kicking in. If you don't feel like going for that 4 mile run, tell yourself you will only go a half-mile. See how you feel, chances are you will finish your *whole* run once you start.

6. **Common Sense.** Don't run ten miles today, if you have not exercised in 15 years. If you haven't had a vegetable in a while, don't load yourself with a meal of only salad and mixed vegetables. In both cases, you will be sorry that you did. Instead, start slow and move gradually towards your health objectives. Small, steady progress is much better than trying to change everything at once. Think of New Years resolutions; they don't work for the long haul because you are trying to change *everything* at once.

7. **Avoid Excuses.** We all have them; they are very good reasons to not work this plan. "I work too hard." "I'm too busy." "I don't have the energy." There are probably hundreds more. They are all just nonsense. Whenever you allow yourself to fall victim to an excuse, you are moving away from victory and moving towards defeat. There is an Arab proverb that says, "He who has health, has hope. And he who has hope has everything." Physical health is so important to the overall quality of life, that you simply can't ignore it. It will help you in *every* area of your life and in this program. Therefore, no excuses, Period!

8. **Get Back Up.** I can guarantee that there will be times when you lose sight of this principle. It may be a day, a week or a month. It has happened to the most health conscious of us and it *will* happen to you. It's okay to indulge occasionally, but if you fall off your program, get back on it as soon as you can. Missing a day of exercising or eating fast food once in a while won't kill you, but continued behavior like this will definitely affect the way you feel. This will have an overall negative effect on your life and your success.

See Action Step #11

SLEEP!

Your body *needs* rest! The "experts" recommend six to eight hours a night. I recommend whatever your body needs. It has become a "badge of honor" in our society to push yourself beyond your limits. I hear people boasting all of the time about their lack of sleep and I can't help but think to myself how foolish they are. Your body *needs* sleep. Your mind *needs* sleep.

I understand that there may be times in the short term, when you may have to put in some extra work time or emergencies may develop which prevent you from getting a good night sleep, but they should be the exception. Take care of whatever pressing issue is at hand and get yourself back on a normal sleep schedule.

I know that I sometimes experience periods where I cannot fall asleep. These periods may be caused by stress or worry; we all experience them; if they last more than a couple of days though I must find a solution. Usually, for me, deep breathing exercises do the trick.

Sleep helps our bodies recover from the stress of work and exercise. It also helps the mind process the information it has received throughout the day. It helps the immune system fight off sickness and disease. Adequate sleep will help you achieve peace and balance in your life. You need to make sure you are getting *enough* rest. Don't let others keep you from a good night's sleep by the promise of "excitement."

To make sure you are getting enough rest, find a time when you can go to bed without putting on the alarm clock, then just sleep until you wake up. Figure out how long you slept; that is probably the amount of time you need. Going forward, learn to get to bed early enough so that you don't need to be woken up by an alarm. If you are worried about oversleeping, just set the alarm for a later time, just in case you oversleep.

See Action Step #12

Conclusion

With the success you are developing in your life, you are also gaining more responsibility. It is becoming more and more your responsibility to bring these principles into other people's lives and into the world in general. It becomes your duty to give back, as your health improves, little by little. You must maintain your strength and continue to bring good into the world, by your influence. ""If you have raced with men on foot and they have worn you out, how can you compete with horses? If you stumble in safe country, how will you manage in the thickets...?"[98] This journey for better health will make you better able to handle your life's mission. Try it. You won't be disappointed! "So don't sit around on your hands! No more dragging your feet! Clear the path for long-distance runners so no one will trip and fall, so no one will step in a hole and sprain an ankle. Help each other out. And run for it!"[99]

Summary

- Take Care Of You
- Two Forces That Work Together
- The Benefits Of A Healthy Lifestyle
- Physical Activity
- Types Of Physical Activity
- Movement
- Play
- What Should My Diet Consist Of?
- The Way To Make Sense Of Your Food
- Twelve Tips For Eating Right
- Other Things For Health
- Create A Plan
- Stick To Your Plan
- Sleep!

Prayer for Health

Lord Teach me about true and lasting health. Help me to see opportunities for healthy choices in the things I do and in who I am on a daily basis.

Amen.

For this Principle say this prayer often and sincerely. Memorize it or put it into your own words if you would like.

Action Steps for Health

Action Step 1 – Take Care Of You

If you are not taking care of yourself by eating right, exercising and doing the other things outlined in this principle then at some lever you don't think very highly of yourself.

For this exercise answer the following questions:

1. Why do you deserve to live a healthy lifestyle?

   _____

   _____

   _____

2. What have you been doing to yourself, or not doing for yourself that may be interfering with your health?

   _____

   _____

   _____

3. How do you plan to change the things listed in #2 above?

   _____

   _____

   _____

4. As you begin the Principle of Physical Health, what are your thoughts, ideas and feelings about taking care of you?

   _____

   _____

   _____

Action Step 2 – Benefits Of A Healthy Lifestyle

In this Action step you will begin living a healthy lifestyle. Review the 10 benefits to a healthy lifestyle (starting on page 176 and the expanded list on page 177):

Answer the following questions:

1. Which of these benefits do you want?

   _____

   _____

   _____

2. Why do you want these benefits?

   _____

   _____

   _____

3. What is one thing you can do today to achieve the benefits you desire?

   _____

   _____

   _____

4. What are your thoughts, ideas and feelings about the benefits of a healthy lifestyle?

   _____

   _____

   _____

Action Step 3 – The 30-Day Challenge

In this Action Step you will set yourself up for the 30-Day Challenge. Accept the 30-day challenge by exercising at least 3 to 4 days a week (more if you prefer) for 30 days. The exercise should consist of cardio, strength, flexibility and agility training.

Do the following activities:

1. For your strength training will you go to a gym or do body weight exercise at home?

   _____

   _____

   _____

2. What are 3 different cardio exercises that you can do?

   _____

   _____

   _____

3. Find an on-line flexibility/stretching guide or get one from the bookstore. Which stretches are you going to perform (remember to stretch each muscle group)?

   _____

   _____

   _____

4. What are 2 or 3 different activities that you can participate in for your agility training?

   _____

   _____

   _____

5. What are your thoughts, ideas and feelings about the 30-Day Challenge?

_____

_____

_____

_____

_____

_____

_____

_____

_____

_____

_____

_____

_____

_____

_____

_____

_____

_____

_____

_____

_____

_____

_____

_____

_____

_____

_____

_____

Action Step 4 – Play

Today's Action Step requires that you play! Play something fun. No, I don't mean playing video games or board games, but play a game that requires you to move. Play a game of tag or dodge ball or whatever else you want.

Do the following activities:

1. What do you want to play?

_____

_____

_____

2. Do you need anyone else to play this? If so, who?

_____

_____

_____

After you're done, answer these questions:

3. Was it fun? How come?

_____

_____

_____

4. Wouldn't it be nice to feel this way every day?

_____

_____

_____

5. What is something you can do to make sure you get playtime every day?

_____

_____

_____

6. What are your thoughts, ideas and feelings about playing?

_____

_____

_____

_____

_____

_____

_____

_____

_____

_____

_____

_____

_____

_____

_____

_____

_____

_____

_____

_____

Action Step 5 – Make Sense Of Your Food

This Action Step will allow you to see exactly what you are eating so that you can learn to make sensible decisions.

Do the following activities:

1. For the next 24 hours, record **_EVERYTHING_** that you eat or drink.

   _____

   _____

   _____

   _____

   _____

   _____

Next, for each item in number one, place it into one of the following categories:

- Water:_____
- Fruits/Vegetables:_____
- Meat:_____
- Breads/Grains/Cereals:_____
- Sugary Snacks: _____
- Non-Sugary Snacks:_____

2. Analyze the list and get familiar with your diet. You will be making changes shortly, so it is important to get familiar with what you're currently doing. What do you notice?

_____

_____

_____

3. What are your thoughts, ideas and feelings about your findings concerning your eating behaviors?

_____

_____

_____

_____

_____

_____

_____

_____

_____

_____

_____

_____

_____

_____

_____

_____

_____

_____

_____

_____

Action Step 6 – Twelve Tips For Eating Right

In this Action Step you need to review the list of "Twelve Tips For Eating Right" starting on page 185.

Once you have reviewed that list, answer the following questions:

1. Which of these tips do you currently use?

_____

_____

_____

2. Which of these tips are you currently not using?

_____

_____

_____

3. Pick two tips from question #2?

_____   _____

4. What, specifically, will you do to incorporate these tips from questions #3 into your eating habits?

_____

_____

_____

5. What are your thoughts, ideas and feelings about eating right?

_____

_____

_____

_____

_____

Action Step 7 – Laugh Hard And Often

This Action Step requires you to laugh. It is a very simple activity that enhances life but too many of us get caught up with the busyness of life and we miss so much joy.

To complete the Action Step answer these questions:

1. Did you laugh yet today? If no, why not?

_____

_____

_____

2. Even if you laughed today, what are you going to do today to laugh even more?

_____

_____

_____

3. What can you do to help make someone else laugh? Who is it?

_____

_____

_____

4. What can you do to make sure you laugh every day (buy a joke book, sign up to receive a daily joke by email, etc.) and help someone else to laugh?

_____

_____

_____

5. What are your thoughts, ideas and feelings about laughing hard and often?

_____

_____

_____

_____

_____

_____

_____

_____

_____

_____

_____

_____

_____

_____

_____

_____

_____

_____

_____

_____

_____

_____

_____

_____

_____

_____

_____

_____

_____

Action Step 8 – Fasting

For this Action Step you will fast for a period of 24 hours, or more if you have experience with fasting. For the next 24 hours consume only water. Record how you feel and what you experience physically, mentally and spiritually, before during and after your fast.

Do the following activities:

1. Before beginning your fasting period record how you feel physically, mentally and spiritually.

   _____

   _____

   _____

2. Halfway through your fasting period (12 hours for a 24 hour fast) record how you feel physically, mentally and spiritually.

   _____

   _____

   _____

3. At the end of your fasting period record how you feel physically, mentally and spiritually.

   _____

   _____

   _____

4. What are your thoughts, ideas and feelings concerning fasting?

_____

_____

_____

_____

_____

_____

_____

_____

_____

_____

_____

_____

_____

_____

_____

_____

_____

_____

_____

_____

_____

_____

_____

_____

_____

_____

_____

Action Step 9 – Effective Breathing

For this Action Step you are going to do some breathing exercises as discussed on page 193.

Follow these simple instructions:

1. Find the correct time for each breath, remembering to keep each breath in the proper ratio of inhale 1 count, hold 4 counts and exhale 2 counts. If you are in excellent health, you should be able to inhale for 5 seconds, hold for 20 seconds and exhale for 10 seconds. Take several practice breaths to determine the correct time and record it here:

   _____

   _____

   _____

2. Do 10 of these breaths now and record how you feel.

   _____

   _____

   _____

3. Determine when you will do these throughout the day. Remember to do them at least 3 times per day.

   _____

   _____

   _____

4. What are your thoughts, ideas and feelings about effective
    breathing?

    _____

    _____

    _____

    _____

    _____

    _____

    _____

    _____

    _____

    _____

    _____

    _____

    _____

    _____

    _____

    _____

    _____

    _____

    _____

    _____

    _____

    _____

    _____

    _____

    _____

Action Step 10 – Create A Plan

In this Action Step you are going to create a personalized plan for your physical health. It will include both exercise and diet plans. As your knowledge grows in this area you will be able to make your plans as detailed as you would like. For now, we will keep it very basic.

Answer the following questions:

1. What types of exercise will you perform on the following days? Remember to include strength, cardio, flexibility and agility training. Do 2 or 3 of these types of exercise per day. Remember to schedule 1 or 2 days off too.

Monday:_____

_____

Tuesday:_____

_____

Wednesday:_____

_____

Thursday:_____

_____

Friday:_____

_____

Saturday:_____

_____

Sunday:_____

_____

For the following, review the "Twelve Tips for Eating Right" starting on page 185.

2. What types of foods do you eat on a regular basis that are harmful to you?

_____

_____

_____

3. What types of foods do you eat on a regular basis that are beneficial to you?

_____

_____

_____

4. As you embark on this new program for physical health, what are your thoughts, ideas and feelings?

_____

_____

_____

_____

_____

_____

_____

_____

_____

_____

_____

_____

_____

_____

Action Step 11 – Stick To Your Plan

For this Action Step you are going to review the list of items in the section, "Stick To Your Plan" starting on page 195. This is necessary even if you currently are sticking to your plan because the day will come when you won't want to. It's better to plan ahead so that you won't be caught off guard.

Do the following activities:

1. Which of these items do you think will help you stay on track when you don't feel like following your program of physical health? Why?

   _____

   _____

   _____

2. Why is it important to stick to your plan even on days that you don't want to?

   _____

   _____

   _____

3. What actions can you take right now to be sure you will follow through even when you don't want to?

   _____

   _____

   _____

4. What are your thoughts, ideas and feelings about sticking to your plan?

_____

_____

_____

_____

_____

_____

_____

_____

_____

_____

_____

_____

_____

_____

_____

_____

_____

_____

_____

_____

_____

_____

_____

_____

_____

_____

_____

_____

_____

Action Step 12 – Sleep

In this Action Step you are going to make sure you're getting enough sleep.

Do the following activities:

1. Find a time when you can go to sleep without setting an alarm to wake you up. Just sleep until you get up naturally. How long did you sleep?

   _____

   _____

   _____

2. Over the course of the next week, go to sleep 20 minutes earlier each night, until you are waking up the following morning without an alarm clock. What time do you need to go to sleep in order to wake up naturally?

   _____

   _____

   _____

3. What would you be able to do if you were better rested? How would your life improve?

   _____

   _____

   _____

4. What are your thoughts, ideas and feelings about getting enough sleep?

   _____

   _____

   _____

   _____

   _____

The Principle of Money

If a person gets his attitude toward money
straight, it will help straighten out almost
every other area in his life. ~~ Billy Graham

Of what use is money in the hand of a fool, since he has
no desire to get wisdom? Proverbs 17:16 (NIV)

It is my belief, that any program of success would be incomplete without a discussion about money and finances or more commonly referred to, as economics. I am not including this principle because money is a measure of success, but because if we learn to manage and use our money *correctly*, we can do so much good with it for ourselves, the people in our lives and the world around us. Many people *wrongly* equate having a lot of money with being successful. I can point out many people who have more money than they can ever possibly spend in a lifetime, but their life is a complete mess. I can also look at many people who have no money at all, but are extremely successful in every other area of their lives. These are the extremes of course and there is a balance. By practicing and learning about *this* principle, as well as the other principles in this program, I am sure you will strike a balance. In fact, I am bold enough and confident enough to claim that you should and could have *all* the money that you need and want.

I am going to give you a very *short* economics lesson. Don't worry, I won't bore you with the unnecessary complication. In fact, the entire lesson will be no more than a few short paragraphs.

A Brief Economics Lesson

Economics is defined, by dictionary.com, as the science that deals with the production, distribution and consumption of goods and services, or the material welfare of humankind.

Another way of defining economics is that it is the *effective* use of scarce resources. I believe and know that, although some resources may be scarce, the money needed to purchase these resources is *not* in short supply.

Poor people need more money. Rich people want more money. Those in the middle, economically, can benefit from having more money. It is human nature and perfectly okay to want more money. In fact, I have *never* met anybody who told me they wanted *less* money. With that said, we need to look at the big picture.

Money and finances are a huge part of *everyone's* life. The food we eat, the electricity in our homes and our family vacations all depend on having money. The luxuries that we enjoy such as the car we drive, or the video game systems we play are determined by it as well. Let's face it; nobody except a very close friend, or family member is just going to give you this stuff for free. You *need* money! Because of this, we need to pay *very* close attention to the money flowing in and out of our pockets. If we don't, then we spend life struggling economically and miss the full potential of our life because of the fear and stress associated with living in lack or want.

If you were to select one hundred people randomly at age sixty-five and look at their financial picture, a snap shot on their life, you will see the following results: one will be "rich" financially; four will be "financially independent"; five will still have to work; fifty four will be broke; and the rest will be dead.

Why is that? These people all started at the same point. None of them had any advantages over the others. Yet, only five out of a hundred people, or five percent of our population ever reach a point of financial independence. Why do so many people fail financially? We *all* have the same chances and opportunities.

Many people *simply* have wrong thinking when it comes to money. There are many reasons for this. There are too many to list, but it can be anything from growing up in an environment of lack, to the thousands of marketing messages we receive every day that tell us and teach us to go and spend *everything* we have, then we'll be happy. In this principle, we will break whatever barrier may be stopping you from having *more* money. For now though, let's get clear on what we want, or think we may want.

See Action Step #1

What must we do in order to change the financial aspect of our life from one of struggle, fear and lack into having what we need and want? The first step in the process is to uncover where we are *presently*. Many of us, up to this point, have *accepted* our financial circumstances as the way it should be. We have thought we deserved our current circumstance and have not attempted to change them.

Common Money Mistakes

I have found that most people make the following mistakes when it comes to building wealth or accepting money into their lives:

1. **They never make having abundance a *necessity*:** If you want something bad enough, you will get it.

Unfortunately, for many of us, we have decided on a comfort level in our lives when it comes to money. We saw how much our parents made, we see how much our friends make and we get comfortable in that range. Instead, look back to the first action step you did in this principle and concentrate on making that amount a *must* have, not a wish, but a *must*.

2.   They associate negative feelings to having money: Many people think negatively about having abundance and they don't even *know* it. This is usually caused by the programming we received as children. You might think, in your mind, that in order to have a lot of money you will have to work too hard to enjoy it. You might have been taught phrases such as: "money doesn't grow on trees," or "money is the root of all evil." That last one needs to be corrected *before* we go any further. The entire phrase is actually read, "For the *love* of money is the root of all evil..."[100] You may have learned that in order to have money, you must take advantage of other people, or that if you make a lot of money you won't be spiritual.

3. They are not generous with what they do have: We live in a society that teaches selfishness and self-centeredness. We are taught to "look out for number one." This causes our *own* brains to reason that there is lack in the world and that we therefore must protect the little that we do have or else we will lose it. Generosity, for most people, has come down to throwing our spare change into the bucket outside the grocery store or the offering plate at church. These fears hold us back from the *true* joy that accompanies giving.

4.   They don't allow themselves to receive: We are taught at a very young age to be self-supporting. We want to be self-made and it hurts our pride to accept something from other people. Even people who give generously, find it difficult to accept the other side of the coin. However, giving and receiving work side-by-side. In fact, if you are always giving, but never receiving, then you are hurting somebody else's chance to experience the *joy* of giving.

5.   They never plan an effective strategy to make money: Most people never learn *how* to attract money into their lives. They never develop the discipline needed to save on a consistent basis. Even among those who do make an attempt to become successful at saving, they never learn to invest the money they do have to attract *more* money into their lives. Just like any other area of life, without having a plan, you will never make much progress. It is like trying to drive a car without a steering wheel. Yes, if you hit the gas pedal you will go *somewhere*, but where you end up is anybody's guess.

6.   **They don't follow a plan, if established:** Most of us never really make much progress in achieving financial success because we never put a plan into action. The few, who are able to put a *realistic* plan together, soon find that their wants and desires simply override their plan. That new, shiny car looks much better in the driveway, than putting $500 a month in to an investment or savings plan. The good intentions are there, but the *discipline* to follow through quickly fades.

7.   **They get comfortable when things start going well:** We *all* do it, when things start going well; we forget to do the simple things that started us moving in the direction of success. It happens in all areas of life too, not just our finances. We procrastinate taking the positive steps that we were *once* making. We begin to spend the money that we were once saving and to make foolish decisions with our money. I would do this; I would go through periods of "famine and feast." It took me a very long time to learn why this was happening. During the periods of "feast," I would quickly forget the struggles I had endured only a short time earlier.

8.   **They allow a financial problem to become a financial disaster:** We all have the *small* bumps in the road that cause us to stumble financially. Maybe it was being away from work for a while or maybe it was an unexpected expense, such as a car repair, or a new furnace that threw us off our plan. When these things happen, we need to pay very close attention to our actions and attitudes. We have to make sure that these *minor* problems do not begin to spiral out of control. It is very easy to turn negative when these things happen and lose focus on the big picture. There was a week, several years ago, when I had two cars needing major repairs, a broken washing machine and a broken furnace. These things *will* happen!

9.   **They rely on financial experts:** We have discussed this in some of the other principles. Do Not *Rely* On Experts! It's okay to get some opinions, but make sure the decision is *yours*, based on *your* circumstances.

10. **They don't trust and rely upon God:** Stop trying to do it *yourself*! It's much easier to ask God to step in and help you with a difficult situation, than it is to try and run the show yourself. Unfortunately, most people never turn to God because our pride and our ego tell us to be self-sufficient. This causes misery and lack of fulfillment. In the remainder of this principle I am going to be discussing *His* plan and how you can adapt it and incorporate it into *your* life. It may not be what you wanted, but it works and it works well!

Take some time right now and review the common money mistakes.

See Action Step #2

What Are Your Beliefs About Money?

I meet many people who are *confused* about money. They know that they need it and they know that having more of it will help to make life easier, but when asked about their beliefs concerning money, they draw a blank. We *all* have beliefs about money, many of which, we are probably unaware of. Yes, we think we want more, but at the subconscious level we are extremely conflicted.

I recently came across a short story that I feel captures the true nature of most people's beliefs about money: "I was starting a new job for a corporation. I was good at what I did for a living. The personnel manager and I were down to the details of employment, and he asked me how much money I believed I deserved. I thought about it and came up with a figure of $400 a month. This was back in the sixties. I didn't want to ask for too much, so I decided to ask for the smallest amount I could live with. He hired me and gave me what I asked for. Later on, when I left that job, the personnel manager told me he had been willing to pay me whatever I wanted. Had I asked for $600 or even $700 a month, which was a tremendous salary at that time, I would have gotten it. I had limited myself by what I believed I deserved."[101]

Many times, I encounter people who just think that it is plain wrong to have more money in their lives. They reason that, with all of the poverty and suffering in the world, it should be unthinkable to expect or ask for more. So, is having more money right or wrong? I believe the answer to that question is: It *depends*. It depends on what you are going to do with it. If it's meant to be used to enrich your life and the world around you, then yes, you should and can have more. It is no different than wanting more spirituality, better relationships, more friends, more intelligence or anything else you can think of.

Another problem that I encounter is that many people think that an *abundant* amount of money is bad or wrong. It's not the money itself; it's the *love* of money that is wrong. "For the love of money is a root of all kinds of evil. Some people, eager for money, have wandered from the faith and have pierced themselves with many griefs."[102]

Money in the *right* hands (yours?), can do much good if kept in the proper perspective. Money itself is *neither* good nor evil. It is simply something used to get us the things we need or want. It is, many times, traded for our time or our ability to perform specified tasks.

Some people believe that money equals power. In the *short* run this may possibly be true. Some people, with a lot of money, get almost everything that they want. "Whoever loves money never has money enough; whoever loves wealth is never satisfied with his income."[103] The long-term effects of this thinking usually lead to self-destruction and an eventual loss of the money that once bought the "power" that was sought. Think of the billionaire stockbrokers, who *eventually* get themselves arrested for cheating the system and trying to gain more "power" for themselves. It can also be seen in the politician, who eventually is brought up on charges for using their office to gain what isn't theirs.

There are also people who believe that there is a shortage of money. I am going to let you in on a little "secret": There is *no* shortage of money! Yes, there may be a shortage in your life, but there is not a shortage here on earth. Many of us simply received bad information about money. The lessons we learned weren't true. When we got money, we were *taught* to hide it under our mattress or do whatever we could to protect it because one day we may run out. So we have, up to this point, been foolish with our decisions about money. It has become a self-fulfilling prophesy in our lives. Those who *have* money, even if they don't deserve it, are not stopping us from getting more. *We* are stopping ourselves from getting more. We don't need to be bitter towards people who have enough; it only hurts us to feel that way. Take a look back at the figure you wrote down for Action Step #1. Do you believe it? *Really?*

Some people *believe* that they don't deserve more money in their lives. On some level, we have been *conditioned* to expect a certain amount of money in our lives, no more, no less. It is a point that we are comfortable with. The funny thing is, that most of us, without realizing it, will work extremely hard to keep ourselves at that level of wealth, which we *think* we deserve. If we are falling short on that amount, then suddenly we will do things, without realizing it, to bring more money into our lives. It's interesting to note, that this work's the other way too. I have seen many people who start bringing more money into their lives. They start making really smart, wise money decisions, then suddenly, again without realizing it, they begin to undermine themselves and they end up right back in that *familiar* comfort zone.

See Action Step #3

Develop A Plan Of Action And Stick To It.

Up to this point, I have discussed the reasons *why* you don't have the money you need or want in your life. I am sure that it has been revealing. Now, let's start talking about *how* to get that money flowing in and through your life.

We spend much of our lives chasing after money, usually with little or no success. The problem is, that we have not equipped or prepared ourselves to receive success in this important area of our lives. That is exactly what we will be doing now.

You must realize, if you do not have the money or financial success you want, it is because you have not equipped or prepared yourself to receive it. You must develop and stick to an *effective* plan for creating wealth.

See Action Step #4

I have identified ten areas that need to be examined and fixed, where necessary. These areas need to be *focused* on in order to bring more money into your life:

1.   Effective Work

2.   Cheerful Tithing

3.   Grateful Receiving

4.   Disciplined Saving/Investing

5.   Eliminating Debt

6.   Wise Decisions

7.   Material Wants (Buy yourself nice things)

8.   Being Content

9.   Weathering Storms

10.   Trusting God

I will examine these ten points and help you to *develop* an effective plan for each of them. Once you are able to do that, it is only a matter of time before you begin to reap the benefits. It is also important to note that, "money is only a tool. It will take you wherever you wish, but it will not replace you as the driver."[104]

Effective Work

There are many people who are poor and lack success in their finances because they are taken advantage of, exploited or oppressed, but one of the reasons I know that people will always struggle with money is because they are lazy and indifferent toward their work. We have heard that, "...For even when we were with you, we gave you this rule: 'If a man will not work, he shall not eat.'"[105] I think that this can be taken even further to say if a man will not work, he shall have nothing to enjoy and share with his loved ones. There will be no success. The world is not a fair place; we all know that, but many people never achieve success in the area of finances because they have not learned to work effectively.

The whole subject of work can be broken down into the following four categories: Honest work, Smart work, Fulfilling work and Moderate work (not "hard" work).

In another Principle, I talk about pursuing your vision, which you will be able to do. For the short term, I suggest continuing to do your current work or to start doing something if you currently aren't. You can apply all of these categories and create change for yourself and others immediately. You can be a positive force right now.

Honest Work

Let's begin with honest work. This, to some of us, seems like a "no-brainer." Work has been with us from the beginning of time and it always will be. "The LORD God took the man and put him in the Garden of Eden to work it and take care of it."[106] The truth is, so many people struggle in this area. They don't *realize* the harm that they are doing to themselves and their finances, by trying to leave a little early, without anyone noticing or spending a little extra time on their lunch break. They are unaware that when they avoid their *responsibilities* or pass them on to someone else that there is damage being done in their *own* financial life. It was Grover Cleveland who said, "Honor lies in honest toil." Stop trying to cut corners and start doing what you are *supposed* to do. By doing this, you will see changes in *all* areas of your life.

When you are working, put everything you have into it. Focus on what you are doing and don't let yourself get distracted by the other areas of your life. "Whatever your hand finds to do, do it with all your might..."[107] That means putting in an honest day. Don't try to get out of your responsibilities. If it is part of your current job, then do it. Do it with a *good* attitude. *Avoid* the negativity and bitterness so many people have toward their work.

This applies no matter what you are currently doing. Through the practice of this program, you will learn how to make positive changes, in *all* areas of your life. This includes your work. If you have a job, it doesn't matter what it is, don't be ashamed or embarrassed by it. There is *honor* in what you are doing. In fact, "All hard work brings a profit, but mere talk leads only to poverty."[108] So, if you are providing for yourself, your family, and the needs of others, hold your head up and know you are doing the right thing.

It's time to look at your work habits and see if you are doing honest work. If you find that you are not, see where corrections need to be made. If you are, congratulate yourself, but also remember to keep it up.

See Action Step #5 - Part 1

Smart Work

Next, I would like to discuss smart work. The most important thing to remember, about what we call smart work, is to have a *plan*. I have found far too many people who do not make a plan for the work that they do to compliment the rest of their lives. They spend their days working, but they never get anywhere.

The first part of the plan is to choose work that *compliments* your health. Do work that requires movement. Whether it is lifting things, walking, or being able to get up throughout your work time to move around, do something that is more than exercise for your fingers at a computer keyboard. Also, do work that does not have a high stress level. This will *help* to keep the rest of your life in balance.

The next thing to consider in developing a plan to do smart work is to choose work that gives you a stake or share in the *success* of the venture. There are many ways to do this, but the one I find is best, is to work for yourself. "The plans of the diligent lead to profit as surely as haste leads to poverty."[109] Diligent, or well-planned decisions are *key* to being able to do this. I do not recommend quitting your job and starting your own company tomorrow, but instead develop a plan and *gradually* move out of what you are currently doing and into a well planned business. Yes, I know that more than fifty percent of businesses fail in the first year, but I suspect this is because the people starting these businesses were not diligent.

Henry Ford once said, "The man who has the largest capacity for work *and* thought is the man who is bound to succeed."[110] Notice that he didn't just mention the capacity for work, but also included thought. I am going to use a simple example to illustrate my point and prove that working for yourself is much smarter than working for someone else. Suppose you are currently earning one thousand dollars a week at your job. If you lost that job tomorrow, you would be out one thousand dollars a week. That could be devastating financially. Now, let's look at an alternative. Imagine that you worked in your own company and you had one hundred customers or clients, who paid you ten dollars a week for your service. If one of those customers "fires" you, there is still nine hundred and ninety dollars left each week.

I know that this goes against conventional wisdom, that says, working for yourself is too risky, but look at the *facts*. It is far less risky than trusting your finances to someone else. The key, though, is to do it slowly.

It would be nice to go in tomorrow and quit your job, but I don't recommend that. Instead, stay where you are and begin to work your business part time. Plan time, every day, to work on and in *your* business. It may be challenging, but do it. Once the money you are making in your business is enough to cover your living expenses, it's *time* to move full time into your venture. At this point, you are no longer able to afford going to your job.

Smart work requires you to *involve* those closest to you, so as not to hurt your relationships. By working with your *spouse*, in your business, you are developing a common purpose that you can both work toward achieving. The alternative is spending a lot of lonely time, trying to get your project off the ground. My wife and I routinely use our time in the car to have a business meeting or we take the kids to the park while we talk about our next move.

The next component of smart work is to find something you *love* to do. I go into much more detail about this in the Principle of Vision, but for now it is okay to start thinking about it. For me it was a pretty natural progression to start a Family Coaching organization based on my desire to help other people and knowing that we have a successful family.

See Action Step #5 - Part 2

Fulfilling Work

I recently came across a very interesting study. The research was done to find the level of job satisfaction in various countries. There were some interesting results; not surprising, but interesting. In the United Sates, more than ninety-five percent of *all* people hated their work. Even in Japan, where workers once stayed with one company for their entire working life, more than seventy-two percent now claim they are dissatisfied with the work they do. This is obviously a growing problem, but it doesn't have to be for you. You are different. You have decided to make changes.

So, what is the key to finding *satisfaction* in your work? Well, the answer is quite simple. You need to be doing work you love. Andrew Carnegie said it best, when he said, "To succeed, you must love what you do."[111] Let's look at why this is true. If you hate your work, you are probably only doing the minimum to get by. It may seem like you are working hard, but you are simply going through the motions. This is not fair to you and it's not fair to the person you are working for. "One who is slack in his work is brother to one who destroys."[112] Many people who hate their work find it easy to do the things I talked about not doing in the section about honest work. I also dealt with this when I worked for other people, doing work that wasn't enjoyable, the lack of enthusiasm during the week, the temptation to "call in sick," the unhappy faces and the fatigue. It's interesting how all of these disappear on the days we get to do the things we enjoy.

To begin doing work you love takes planning and thought. As I mentioned earlier, don't quit your job tomorrow and go out and buy that infomercial plan for making millions overnight just yet. This is what many people do and that is *why* most businesses fail. Some of these are real money making opportunities, but most of them are scams. Besides, you are looking for work that you love to do, not to go and make a million dollars overnight.

You need to find work that *excites* you; something that you are passionate about. When I was developing this program and somebody asked me about it, I would be able to talk to them for hours about it. Helping others is just something I feel very strongly about. In fact, I did it at my church and through other organizations for many years without any type of compensation. I just loved to do it. You need to find something that you just *love* to do.

When you start to discover what you are passionate about and begin to take steps to turn it into an opportunity to make money, you will have more energy, more happiness and more fulfillment. "A man can do nothing better than to eat and drink and find satisfaction in his work. This too, I see is from the hand of God, for without him who can eat or find enjoyment."[113] By doing this, you will also *start* to make progress on the Principle of Vision, which we will be discussing soon. You will give yourself a head start into uncovering and pursuing this critical element of your life.

The truth is, when you find work you love to do and you have enthusiasm, passion and purpose, YOU CAN NOT FAIL! I see it again and again; people moving out of work they hate, into work they love. These people transform their finances for the positive, sometimes quicker than can even be imagined.

See Action Step #5 - Part 3

Moderate Work

We have discussed honest work, smart work and fulfilling work. The last component of effective work is moderation. Work is a *necessary* part of life. It helps to give us direction and purpose. Just think back to a day when you had a good day at work. It's satisfying. Work is good! It's even better when you are doing the things suggested here. So let's be clear about work. It's overworking that is the problem. Even God rested after doing the work of creating the world and we are given instructions to not overwork.[114]

We all know *someone* who spends too much time working. In fact, I know people who work three jobs and they are still broke. The sad thing is that in their quest for "more," they are destroying everything else in their life. These people have lost sight of why they are working in the first place. We all work for money, that is clear, but when you begin to spend too much time working, your relationships suffer, your personal life suffers, your health suffers and your *finances* suffer.

If you have fallen into the trap of overworking, I urge you to become *free* today. Take some time off to spend with family or friends. Do some exercise or start to spend some time enjoying a hobby that you have become too busy to participate in. If you like, just take some time to rest.[115] If you have been overworking for a long time, you may have forgotten the delight found in simple pleasures. "Over work makes for restless sleep."[116]

You need to enjoy the *fruit* of your labor. In fact, "you will eat the fruit of your labor; blessing and prosperity will be yours."[117] After learning to work in moderation, you will begin to *feel* rejuvenated and more relaxed. Who knows, you might even begin to enjoy some quiet time. So, "have regular hours for work and play; make each day both useful and pleasant and prove that you understand the worth of time by employing it well. Then youth will be delightful, old age will bring few regrets and life will become a beautiful success."[118]

There *will* be times when there may be a lot to do and you find yourself overworking. There are times, when there might be a lot asked of you. These situations are okay if they are the *exceptions* to the rule and not the normal course of your life. Accept moderation in your work and start living the good life today. You should "and to make it your ambition to lead a quiet life: You should mind your own business and work with your hands, just as we told you, so that your daily life may win the respect of outsiders and so that you will not be dependent on anybody."[119]

See Action Step #5 - Part 4

Cheerful Tithing

I am going to take some time, right now, to discuss a very controversial topic. It has become controversial, but it really shouldn't be. I am going to discuss tithing, or the practice of taking ten percent of *everything* you make and giving it away, first, before you do anything else with your money. I am not talking about generosity in general; I am talking about tithing in particular. Tithing is not "generosity." Tithing is *required*. There is an entire principle based on generosity. For now, let's discuss taking the *first* ten percent of *everything* you make and giving it away. I can see those of you who know about tithing with your eyes glazing over, but stick with me now. Those of you who haven't heard about tithing are going to get a very important lesson. It will have a *direct* impact on your future financial prosperity.

Tithing is a *Christian* principle. Christians are taught to "Honor the Lord with your wealth, with the first fruits of all your crops, then your barns will be filled to overflowing, and your vats will brim over with new wine."[120] It is something that everyone *needs* to do in order to get yourself on track with your money and finances. Let's look at some facts about tithing. You will quickly see, that although it is beneficial, it is not commonly practiced:

- Only six percent of people who claim to be Christian actually tithe.

- In the average church, seventeen percent of church attendees say they tithe, but only three percent actually do.

- Forty percent of people will give nothing to their church this year.

- Twenty percent of those who attend church contribute seventy-five percent of the resources.

- Ninety-one percent of people who attend church make more money than they ever have in their life.[121]

- With numbers like these, it's no wonder so many people's financial lives are such a mess. Why are these numbers so bad? Why don't people tithe? I have uncovered four of the main reasons that people don't tithe:

- **Ignorance:** They just don't *know* about it, or they aren't sure if it "works."

- **Fear**: They are fearful that if they give away that ten percent, they won't have enough to live on.
- **Greed**: They just want more of everything and are unwilling to give it up.
- **Uncertainty**: They just don't think their small amount will make a difference, or have an impact.

So what happens when you tithe? How can I confidently stand behind the *promise* that the Bible makes about tithing? "'Bring the whole tithe into the storehouse, that there may be food in my house. Test me in this,' says the Lord Almighty, 'and see if I will not throw open the floodgates of heaven and pour out so much blessing that you will not have room enough for it.'"[122]

You will gain freedom without realizing it; many of us have become slaves of our possessions. Tithing will release you from that burden and you will be able to put what you own in its *proper* prospective.

You will be able to take chances. When you fully grasp the power of tithing, you will begin to realize that you can *trust* the outcome. "Remember this - you can't serve God and money, but you can serve God with money."[123]

You will start on the road towards living a truly generous life. There is an entire Principle of Generosity, but this is where it begins. Tithing is learning to take that first step towards generosity.

Following rules will become easier. If you can get yourself to part with money, then the other principles and rules outlined in this program, will become much *easier* to follow.

You will develop discipline that will spread into *all* areas of your life. Developing the consistent behavior of tithing will help you in saving more money and taking the other actions necessary to bring success into your life.

You will become a better steward of *everything* in your life. You will see that you have been entrusted with resources. It is your responsibility to use those resources correctly. As you improve, you will be trusted with even more.

You will begin to experience financial abundance in your life. By tithing on a consistent basis, you are teaching your brain that there is *more* than enough. When you continue to tithe at higher and higher levels of income, your brain begins to recognize that there really is no shortage and you begin to receive more.

I know that many people need more in their lives; I also know that many people want more in their lives. The answer is in tithing. Learn to tithe and you *will* have more. "Give and it will be given to you. A good measure, pressed down, shaken together and running over, will be poured into your lap. For with the measure you use, it will be measured to you."[124] In other words, learn to tithe and you will have more. Just take this one action and make it a habit, then it will become effortless.

Avoid worrying about if your tithe is *enough*. It is what is happening in the heart and mind that matters most. Some people believe that God only blesses those who give the most. This is entirely wrong thinking. It's not about having a lot of money that makes the difference. If you read the story about the widow's offering,[125] you will clearly see that attitude and willingness are much more important than amount. You do not have to be the one who gives the most or work the hardest to get His attention. Just learn to tithe with the right attitude.

The right attitude consists of being cheerful and not giving reluctantly, but because it is the right thing to do.[126] Make sure that when you give, you are not worrying about what you will get in return. Tithe with no thought of compensation. You should not be expecting to get anything back. So tithe with a *good* attitude and tithe with your heart.

Before I end this section on tithing, I would like to mention a few more things. First, do not listen to advice about tithing from someone who doesn't believe in tithing. "Listen carefully to what I am saying and be wary of the shrewd advice that tells you how to get ahead in the world on your own. Giving, not getting, is the way."[127] You don't have to "claw" your way to the top and you don't have to "look out for number one." You just have to tithe.

Lastly, you may have "tried" tithing in the past and it didn't "work." Maybe you did it for two weeks; maybe even a year. Tithing is not something you do for a little while. It is a *lifetime* commitment. You must tithe when everything is going great; you also must tithe, even when it looks like you can't afford to. You *will* be richly blessed.

See Action Step #6

Grateful Receiving

Many people I speak with are better givers than receivers. What they don't realize, though, is that the two go together; that you can't have one without the other. There are *many* reasons that you should allow yourself to receive. Among them, is the fact that "God has given us two hands; one to receive with and the other to give with. We are not cisterns made for hoarding; we are channels made for giving."[128]

The first thing to realize is that if you have abundance in your life, you *deserve* it. Don't ignore this fact, it is important. It means that you have sown good things into other people's lives and that you are allowing that good to come back to you. In a way, you are being rewarded for the *wise* choices you have made along the way.

Receiving is *evidence* that you are giving. You have planted the seeds and are now reaping the harvest. "Do not be deceived: God cannot be mocked. A man reaps what he sows."[129] Remember, though, when you receive, there is a very good chance that it probably will not come back from the same person you give to or in *your* time frame. If you learn to recognize when it does come back, you will see that this law works *every* time.

Receiving is evidence that you have been a good steward with the resources you have been trusted with. Stewardship is the responsible management, distribution and use of the resources that have been placed in *your* care. When you make good decisions with the resources you currently have, you will be given more. Good decisions generally come once you put money in the proper perspective, so that your mind is not clouded by money. Happiness is not in the mere possession of money; it lies in the joy of achievement, in the thrill of creative effort and the blessing of other people.

Receiving allows you to pass along the gift of giving to someone else. We all know someone who, when asked what they want for Christmas, will respond by saying, something like, "Nothing, keep the money for yourself." When that happens, the one rejecting the gift is not allowing other people to experience the joy and benefits of giving. In a way, the one who will not gratefully receive is being selfish by not allowing others to give. We have all heard that, "...it is more blessed to give than to receive."[130] Think about that for a minute. Don't you want others to be "more blessed?" This happens when you allow them to give and you to receive.

In order for someone to give, someone else must receive; they work *together*. One does not exist without the other. Allow others to give by allowing yourself to receive. You will be helping yourself and other people more than you can imagine. You will also have much more than you can ever imagine. You will be creating value for others and doing good in the world. "Goodness is the only investment that never fails."[131]

See Action Step #7

Disciplined Saving/Investing

It's time to tackle a very troubling habit that we as a society engage in. It causes us much uncertainty and sometimes a great deal of stress. I am talking about the lack of savings and investing that we engage in. "If you would be wealthy, think of saving as well as getting."[132]

The *instant* gratification that we get from buying "stuff" causes us to fall far short of any savings or investing that we need to live a successful life. Let's first look at the facts: As a *society* we actually have a negative saving rate. That means we spend more than we make. *We* did some research and found the following information. In Japan, people on average save 27% of their income. Here in the United States, that amount is actually negative. Our average net worth is around *negative* nine thousand dollars.

We are the richest society on earth, but we still cannot get ourselves to save. To put it another way, we spend about 103% of what we make. We are making foolish decisions and it needs to stop. "The wise have wealth and luxury, but fools spend whatever they get."[133] It's time to begin making *smart* choices and decisions that will lead to success in our finances. We, as a nation, have amassed over $13 billion in debt. This makes your share over $43,000[134]. If you are not in the United States, the best advice I can give is to adopt good habits now before they take you down a road you don't want to be on.

What most people don't realize though is that the solution to creating more wealth in your life is not to just make more money. That helps, but only if you have developed the discipline to save and invest. The solution lies in learning *how* money works. You must learn that by saving a little bit every week or month, you will grow your savings and investments over time.

You *must* be saving and investing at least 10% of your income. You must develop the habit, however painful, in order to begin making real progress. You must take the time to research your saving and investment options so that you are able to make *informed* choices and to stay current about your finances.

Saving and investing serve different purposes, but if you develop the discipline to do one, the ability to do the other should come naturally. Saving money is for the short term, while investing is for the long term. The methods and ideas for helping you achieve success will work interchangeably. You should spread your savings and investments out over *several* different options, "...divide your investments among many places, for you do not know what risks might lie ahead."[135]

It's a known fact that most people save and invest nothing. If they do, it's usually not enough to make any *measurable* difference in their life. The good news is, that even if you have never saved or invested, you can begin right now.

Having savings and investments are important. If you have an emergency fund, car repairs, home expenses or unexpected fees will not become a financial burden. You can also save for things that you want, such as vacations, a new car, a house and college tuition. These can all become a reality when you *learn* to put money aside. You should also be planning for your retirement. Don't rely on other people to take care of you. The bottom line is, that when you do these things, you will find less stress and more success and happiness.

I have included some tips to help you begin saving and investing. There are many different things you can do besides what I have included here, but you can use these ideas to get you started:

- Try using direct deposit, if your employer offers it. The less you handle the money directly, the better off you will be. You can also direct a certain amount to go into savings and investments.

- Some banks have programs where they will round up on purchases and deposit the extra money into a savings account. For example: If you buy a sandwich for $4.50, they will charge you $5.00, but the extra 50 cents will go into your savings account.

- Avoid overpriced "extras" that really don't add value to your life. Make your coffee at home or bring your lunch to work instead of going out.
- Pay yourself an established amount each week or month before you pay your bills and expenses. Do this no matter what. If you wait until everything else is paid, there may be very little for you.
- Wait at least 48 hours after deciding to purchase big-ticket items or sign contracts and obligations before taking action. This will help you decide if you really want or need the item.
- Create a retirement plan. Whether it is a 401K at work or an IRA, get it started and make contributions.
- Make a commitment not to pay full price for anything. Plan your menus based on grocery store sales or wait until that electronics store puts the computer you want in their weekly flyer.

The point is to do simple things that add up over time; these simple things will become habits which will become effortless over time. Before you know it you will be on the road to saving and investing success.

See Action Step #8

Eliminating Debt

Living in debt has become a way of life for many people. In doing this, we have become slaves. Proverbs 22:7 clearly says, "The rich rule over the poor, and the borrower is servant to the lender."[136] Many people today have been fooled by *complex* marketing strategies created by today's mega corporations. We have been fooled into thinking that debt is an acceptable way of life. We have been taught that the way to success and prosperity is through the use of loans or credit cards. In fact many of the advertisements of today make you believe that you are somehow more important or sophisticated if you have their credit card or loan. It doesn't have to be this way.

It was in the early to mid-20th century when a group of people got together and realized that they could sell a bunch of stuff that people don't need to people who don't need it. They further discovered that if they did this successfully, then *they* would be able to buy a bunch of stuff that they didn't need. After doing this for a while, they discovered that the people who couldn't afford stuff were admiring them. This made them feel important. Being ego driven creatures, they decided to figure out a way to sell *more* useless stuff to people who didn't need it so that they could buy more STUFF for themselves. This cycle is repeated endlessly. Welcome to "success" as it stands today. However, this wasn't always the case.

People *used* to work and save for the things they wanted. Yes, it took patience, discipline and time but the things they had were much more valued.

Try missing a payment on one of those loans and see how important and sophisticated you feel. "If you think nobody cares if you're alive, try missing a couple of car payments."[137] It's funny, but it's true. When you sign that loan paperwork for the new car or finance anything else, you are giving up a portion of your life, a part of your freedom.

If you read the Bible, there is not one time where God uses debt to bless *anyone*. When debt is discussed, it is always a burden that drives you into slavery. Always remember, "Debt is the slavery of the free."[138]

Here is what you can do now and in the future, to free yourself from this slavery and move forward. When you eliminate the burden of debt from your life, you will begin to feel the freedom in your life grow minute by minute. I have compiled a list of suggestions, which will help you eliminate this terrible burden now and forever.

- **Live on cash.** It's quite simple. If you don't have cash to pay for it, don't buy it. It's called living *within* your means and it's important. Benjamin Franklin even went so far as to say, "...rather go to bed supperless than rise in debt."[139]

- **Pay more on your credit cards, car loans or other debt than you actually owe.** This will help you pay down your debt much sooner than you would otherwise be able to do. You must be *disciplined*. You may have spent years creating your debt. "Debt is like any other trap; easy enough to get into, but hard enough to get out of."[140]

- **Create a budget and *stick to it*.** There are plenty of online resources geared to this purpose. Some of them have a monthly or annual fee involved and some of them do not. Find one that works for you and use it. "Live within your means; never be in debt, and by husbanding your money you can always lay it out well.

But when you get in debt you become a slave. Therefore I say to you, never involve yourself in debt, and become no man's surety."[141]

- **Create an emergency fund.** Unexpected expenses such as car repairs, broken washing machines or any other unplanned expense make debt accumulate quickly. These things are unavoidable, but you can make sure they don't destroy your financial plan by making sure you have cash on hand for these unplanned expenses.

- **Finally, be patient.** You *will* overcome the debt you have created in your life, but it may take some time. If you don't get discouraged, you will begin to see the light at the end of the tunnel.

As you follow these *new* rules to managing your debt, you will begin to free yourself from the chains of past mistakes and as you free up more and more of your money from the burden of debt, you will see the benefits of being debt free. You will never again want to go back to that horrible place. You will put yourself in a position where, "...God will bless you as He has promised you, and you will lend to many nations, but you will not borrow..."[142]

See Action Step #9

Wise Decisions

It is important for *you* to begin taking responsibility for your current situation. You need to start making wise decisions with your money rather than foolish one's. For an example of what wise decisions will produce in your life I like to point out the story of the talents in the Bible.[143] We all know it (if you don't, I suggest reading it), but few of us have actually thought about the decisions made by the three servants and how they apply in our lives. Basically the two servants who made *wise* decisions with the money entrusted to them were given more, while the servant who made a foolish decision was stripped of all he had. As Dave Ramsey so bluntly puts it, "If you sow stupid, you reap desperate and broke."[144] There are certain things you can begin doing, right now, to help you start making wise decisions with your money *immediately* and therefore begin reaping the good that comes with these decisions.

Part of your new responsibility is to learn about *your* finances. You don't need to learn everything there is to know about economics and money, just what applies to you now. As your situation changes you may need to learn new and different things but don't worry about that now.

Learn about saving and investing, taxes, etc. Learn about your situation so that you can make *informed* choices. You must make your own decisions without the "help" of experts. "By wisdom a house is built, and through understanding it is established; through knowledge its rooms are filled with fare and beautiful treasures."[145]

Next, learn that you *will* make mistakes. That is okay. Mistakes are part of the learning process and the success process. The point is not to get so worried about making mistakes that you become too paralyzed to make a decision or to take action. This is a sure way to fail.

Don't be afraid to make mistakes, but also make sure that you *learn* from those mistakes. Don't be afraid to take risks, but when a risk doesn't turn out as planned, make sure that you readjust. "The prudent see danger and take refuge, but the simple keep going and pay the penalty."[146]

Everybody has heard of baseball's Babe Ruth, because he hit the most home runs, but what most people don't realize is that he also had the most strikeouts. I have made my share of financial mistakes but the one thing I realize is that I will recover even if it seemed painful at the time.

The next suggestion is to find people who are getting the results you want and listen to what they say. It is accepted wisdom that in order to become wealthy, you need to "build a better mouse trap." If you research history's billionaires, you will see how few of them actually invented *anything*. On the other hand, many of the people who *did* invent something seldom struck it rich. What the billionaires did was improve on somebody else's invention or idea. I don't suggest that you spend your life trying to achieve billionaire status. There are far too many more important things in life. The point is that we can all learn from these people.

It is important to note that for this section you should seek someone that you know, who you can actually speak with face to face about their experiences and ideas. This will have a much more concrete impression on you than somebody you don't know.

Next is to adopt *new* beliefs about money. For many of us, having abundance in our life is the unknown. You must condition your mind to receive money into your life and you must do it often and continually. This can be done by visualizing the good that can come from you *having* money. Visualize the positive experiences you can generate with family and friends when you have more. Visualize how life would be better and more fulfilling if money were not an issue. Also, visualize the pain that you experience by not having money. The inability to take vacation, or not being able to buy your child a new toy are some examples.

Also, realize that you have so many good things in your life. When you learn to feel this abundance in other areas of your life it has a way of translating into your finances. You are much wealthier than you think. You simply need to accept that simple truth into your life. The thoughts that you focus on *are* the reality that you will experience.

Finally, be slow to make financial decisions. Think things over, weigh your options. You might miss an *occasional* opportunity, but over the long haul, you will make better, more effective decisions in this area of your life.

See Action Step #10

Material Wants

It is okay for you to have nice things in your life. In fact, it is *important* for you to have nice things. Whether it is a car or a house or any type of luxury item, if you are practicing this program you will have these things. Treat yourself to the things in life that you want. Remember though do not use credit. If you use wisdom and practice stewardship, you will be able to get nice things without credit.

God uses money and material possession to test your faithfulness to Him. In fact, the Bible talks more about money and material possession than it does about Heaven or Hell. How you manage your money and your "stuff" *determines* how much more you will receive. "Whoever can be trusted with very little can also be trusted with much, and whoever is dishonest with very little will also be dishonest with much. So if you have not been trustworthy in handling worldly wealth; who will trust you with true riches? And if you have not been trustworthy with someone else's property, who will give you property of your own?"[147]   Make sure you're keeping your material wants in their proper perspective.

Here are some rules to help keep money and "stuff" in their proper perspective:

- **Don't make acquiring "stuff" your primary reason for existence.** Make sure you have your priorities in order and make sure your *basic* needs are met before you begin to purchase luxury items. I am always amazed when I see the guy driving by in the brand new Mercedes, who lives in a tenement full of cockroaches and rats. Instead, get yourself a nice home and then go buy the car. In fact, I once knew a homeless person who had a beautiful car. I am sure he isn't the only one. If your children need new shoes, don't go out and buy the new big screen TV first. Make sure your priorities are straight. "Don't tell me where your priorities are. Show me where you spend your money and I'll tell you what they are"[148]

- **Don't set your heart on the stuff of life.** "Where your treasure is, there your heart will be also."[149] Our society has become obsessed with acquiring stuff. It has become normal to measure someone's success by the size of their house, the kind of car they drive or how many other luxury items they own. Don't fall into that trap. Be *content* with what you have. Yes, strive for more, but don't let the quest for more stuff become your life's aim. I know of so many people who are letting the good things in life pass them by simply because they are focusing on material possessions.

- **Don't be afraid to sell out to God.** Make God your treasure. This is discussed in other parts of the program, but it should be mentioned here as well. Make God the center of your life and you *will* have the things that you need and want. In Him your wealth is *truly* secure. In other words, stop trying to manage your finances by yourself. "A faithful man will be richly blessed, but one eager to get rich will not go unpunished."[150] Learn to, relax and let Him work in your life; place Him at the center and He will do the rest.

- **Lastly, remember that money has no bearing on what you are worth as a human being.** Whether you make a hundred million dollars a year, own a yacht and live in a mansion or you make ten thousand dollars a year, own a beat up rusted out car and live in a small apartment, we all have the *same* value as people. Don't forget that. Don't love money or your "stuff" more than you love the important things in your life. "For the love of money is a root of all kinds of evil. Some people, eager for money, have wandered from the faith and pierced themselves with many griefs."[151]

See Action Step #11 - Part 1

Being Content

I am sure many of us have looked out at our neighbor's house in envy. There may even have been times when we have gotten jealous at the luxury car that our friend or co-worker drives. When we see these nice possessions of others, many times we begin to imagine the pleasure and satisfaction that must come from owning these luxury items. When this happens we must remember, as hard as it is in the moment that, "contentment makes poor men rich. Discontent makes rich men poor."[152] So how do you maintain contentment in a word that is so focused on material possessions? I have found several things that help.

The first thing to realize is that you are a *spiritual* being. Yes, we exist in a physical world but you will never be able to fix a spiritual deficiency with material objects. You have much deeper needs such as love and an inner desire to grow spiritually. These needs will never be filled by buying "stuff." I know many people who do this and they may even feel satisfied by it for a short time, but *eventually* they will need to buy more things. It leads to a state of mental, physical, spiritual and financial poverty.

Instead, keep yourself focused on what is *truly* important and you will have abundance in your life. Remember, "the richest person is the one who is content with what he has."[153]

The next suggestion is to make sure we are putting money in its *proper* place. Money is only a tool to measure the exchange of goods and services between people. We all need food, clothing and shelter; that's it! Anything beyond that is for our physical comfort and is not necessary for contentment. I'm not saying that it isn't nice to have, but it's not *needed*. Focus on your spiritual needs, instead of material wants. When you start to meet *these* needs your focus will change. As scripture says, "... Man does not live on bread alone, but by every word that proceeds from the mouth of God."[154] If you are not happy and content more money is not the answer. "Money never made a man happy yet, nor will it. The more a man has, the more he wants. Instead of filling a vacuum, it makes one."[155]

Don't compare yourself with other people. You shouldn't do this in *any* area of your life. Your money and finances are no different. When you do this, you begin to feel superior to those you have more than and inferior to those you have less than. It's important to remember that everyone is on their *own* journey. Some people are further along in their journey than others and when you begin to compare, you cause harm to yourself. We all can take a lesson from the parable about the landowner who hired laborers to work in his vineyard.[156] In this story the landowner hires workers for his vineyard and he continues to hire more workers throughout the day. When the day ends and the workers come from the vineyard to be paid, the landowner decides to give each worker the same amount of money, regardless of when they started. Those who worked the longest became mad and asked the landowner about it. He replied, "...Friend, I am not being unfair to you. Didn't you agree to work for a denarius?"[157] The same should be true with you. Don't compare yourself; just keep moving forward.

Make sure you are grateful for what you *do* have. You don't need to be satisfied, but that doesn't mean that you can't show gratitude. I meet so many people who many would say have "made it" financially, but they lack the simple gratitude that makes it all worthwhile. Therefore, they are usually miserable, unhappy and unfulfilled.

"If you want to feel rich, just count the things you have that money can't buy."[158] Always remember, as bad as you think your money situation may be right now, the very fact that you have the resources to go through this program; the money to buy it, the computer to download and print the activity forms, etc. means you are better off than the 95% of the world who don't even know where their next meal may be coming from. Your worst financial nightmare may be someone else's dream come true. "Let your conduct be without covetousness; be content with such things as you have."[159]

See Action Step #11 - Part 2

Weathering Storms

The question isn't *will* I encounter financial storms in my life? The question is what do I do *when* I encounter financial storms? They will come. You need to be ready or else you are setting yourself up for disaster. "Wisdom is a shelter as money is a shelter, but the advantage of knowledge is this: that wisdom preserves the life of it's possessor."[160] Take the time now, to prepare, so that when the storms come, you *will* be ready. By keeping the following information in mind, you will be able to overcome difficulties and even come out stronger.

First, develop a belief that you are more than *anything* that happens to you financially. Prepare a statement or find quotes and scriptures that support this fact. This will help keep you motivated to continue going, even if it looks like your situation may not get better. I like the following: "I know what it is to be in need, and I know what it is to have plenty. I can do everything through Him who gives me strength."[161]

Next, as tempting as it is when things start to get tough, never use credit. This may take some effort and discipline, but you will be much better off, after the storm has passed, if you do not use credit to get you through. It may seem painful at times, but consider the words of Thomas Jefferson in a letter to his daughter: "Be assured that it gives much more pain to the mind to be in debt, than to do without any article whatever which we may seem to want."[162]

Use wisdom in your decisions. I think wisdom, during a financial storm, consists of 3 things, that if done *consistently* will help you weather any storm that may come your way:

Don't gamble. During a storm it is easy to fall for a clever get-rich-quick scheme or to try some other means of getting through the tough time faster. "Greedy people try to get rich quick but don't realize they're headed for poverty."[163] If it sounds too good to be true, it probably is.

Keep Working towards a solution. "Honest labor bears a lovely fact."[164] This is true when things are going great *and* when you are struggling. It's easy to get discouraged in the midst of financial difficulties, but keep your head up and keep pressing on.

Continue to give. Is it hard? Yes! You must keep your spirit of generosity alive even when it seems difficult. "One man gives freely, yet gains even more; another withholds unduly, but comes to poverty. A generous man will prosper; he who refreshes others will himself be refreshed."[165]

Lastly, seek God. In Proverbs it says, "He who trusts in his riches will fall, but the righteous will flourish like foliage." We will be talking more about trusting God with your finances shortly, but for now, just know that to get through a financial storm it is important to stay in *close* contact with Him. So seek Him and pray often.

This leads us to our next and final area of finances and money; trusting God. If you stay focused on the information in this principle, as well as the rest of this program you will be well equipped to weather a financial storm.

See Action Step #12 - Part 1

Trusting God

We don't make money because *we* are smart or have more ability than someone else. We make money because God knows that we *need* it to function in this world. He provides and we are meant to do certain things with that provision. We are trusted to make good decisions and when we do, we are given more. "But remember the Lord your God, for it is he who gives you the ability to produce wealth and so confirms His covenant, which He swore to your forefathers, as it is today."[166]

One of the most harmful traits someone can possess is over reliance on other people. Being *overly* reliant on other's kindness or generosity makes you extremely vulnerable. I believe that God wants everybody, including you, to be God reliant. He hasn't given your ability to produce wealth to someone else such as a long lost relative or a friend who just won the lottery. You don't have to wait for unlikely events like these to occur. You *can* produce wealth today.

When the Israelites became Egypt's slaves for 400 years, they had nothing to call their own. Everything they received came from the "generosity" of their masters. They couldn't improve their lot in life. All their initiative and self-reliance was taken away from them. God however didn't want them to be reliant on others or even self-reliant; he wanted them to be God-reliant, so he led them into the wilderness. Sometimes we are led into our *own* wilderness so that we can become God-reliant.

The freedom from over-reliance on others is a great feeling. It means that you can now follow *God's* plan for your finances without fearing what other people think or say. I am not saying to reject other people's help or generosity. Just don't *depend* on it. Depend on the *promises* of God.

God Is Not Against Us Being Wealthy

"I tell you the truth," Jesus replied, "no one who has left home or brothers or sisters or mother or father or children or fields for me and the gospel will fail to receive a hundred times as much in this present age (homes, brothers, sisters, mothers, children and fields-and with them, persecutions) and in the age to come, eternal life.'[167]

I want to point out that God is not against us attaining wealth. As long as we make sacrifices and give, he will provide us with a hundred-fold return. We don't have to wait until we get to heaven for that hundred-fold return either. The hundred-fold return is "in this present age." We must realize that a hundred-fold return on this earth is a very small reward compared to what we get when we arrive in heaven. That is, eternal life.

Within this scripture, right along with our blessing, we also see Jesus mention that persecution comes along with our reward. There are many people who become jealous when their friends, family and neighbors attain success. They see others becoming successful as their failure. They may even criticize you for obtaining the very things that they themselves want.

Are you responsible enough to be blessed? Blessed people always stir up controversy. They tend to offend those who choose to live in mediocrity. Remember, to him whom much is given, much is required. There is a huge responsibility for those people God chooses to become leaders and builders of faith. Hard work and faith will always lead to success. Success will always lead to controversy and criticism.

Remember this on your journey: "What, then, shall we say in response to this? If God is for us, who can be against us? He who did not spare his own Son, but gave him up for us all-how will he not also, along with him, graciously give us all things?"[168]

"But you, man of God, flee from all this, and pursue righteousness, godliness, faith, love, endurance and gentleness."[169]

As I have established, the pursuit of money at all costs is evil. I have seen the scenario played out so many times. A young family just starting out discovers that they want so many more things than what their current income can support. The husband starts working harder and the wife starts working harder. They see less and less of each other and the kids. This is where the family begins to disintegrate.

The truth is, all that they have to do is stop chasing the money, and ask God for their needs and wants. Of course, they need to ask in a spirit of total faith. They also need to pursue the things of God, rather than the things of the world. These things that are worth pursuing are righteousness, godliness, faith, love, endurance and gentleness. Jesus said that if you seek God, "all these things shall be added unto you."[170]

I spent my early 20's fresh out of college working 15 hours a day, "chasing the money." I always believed in God, but I had the belief that only by working so much would I ever achieve financial success; nothing could be further from the truth. God will take care of you. God will give you all things. He does this when he knows that you are truly seeking Him; not seeking Him just to gain wealth. You must seek the giver, not the gift. Would you want a friend or family member who is more interested in what you can give him or her more than they are in loving you? God feels the same way.

If we know all of this, why is money such a touchy subject and why do we worry so much about it? I believe it is because we trade our time for some amount of money per hour or week or year.

See Action Step #12 – Part 2

Conclusion

Our short study of money and finances has ended. Follow the suggestions outlined in this principle and you *will* achieve financial success and abundance in your life. Learn how to get yourself to follow through on what we have just learned about and you will be successful. Now let's get back to the *really* important material in the other principles.

As with the other Principles, continue to work on improvement in *all* of them and every area of your life will improve. Continue to stay focused on what's important and everything else will fall into place.

Summary

- Common Money Mistakes
- What are your beliefs about Money?
- Develop a plan of action and stick to it.
- Effective Work
    - Honest Work
    - Smart Work
    - Fulfilling Work
    - Moderate Work
- Cheerful Tithing
- Grateful Receiving
- Disciplined Saving/Investing
- Eliminating Debt
- Wise Decisions
- Material Wants
- Being Content
- Weathering Storms
- Trusting God
- God Is Not Against Us Being Wealthy

Prayer for Money

Lord, teach me to be wise with the wealth you have blessed me with. Help me to be generous and content with the things that I have. Show me how to honor you with it as well.

Amen.

Action Steps for Money

Action Step 1 – Get Clear

In this Action Step you will get clear on what amount of money you want and why you deserve it. Do the following activities:

1. Write down an amount of money that you want.

   _____

   _____

   _____

2. Why don't you have this amount of money right now?

   _____

   _____

   _____

3. Why do you deserve it?

   _____

   _____

   _____

4. What are your thoughts, ideas and feelings about the amount of money you deserve?

   _____

   _____

   _____

Action Step 2 – Common Money Mistakes

In this Action Step you are going to get clear on the money mistakes that you are currently making. Which ones do you make? Complete the checklist and then answer the following questions.

1. Review the list of Common Money mistakes that most people make, starting on page 228.

Do You	YES	NO
Make having abundance a necessity?	☐	☐
Associate positive feelings to money?	☐	☐
Give generously with what you do have?	☐	☐
Allow yourself to receive?	☐	☐
Have an effective strategy?	☐	☐
Follow you plan, if you have one?	☐	☐
Continue to follow your plan, even when things are going well? ☐ ☐		
Stay positive, even when you experience financial problems?	☐	☐
Make your own decisions and not rely on experts ☐ ☐		
Trust and rely on God?	☐	☐

2. For any "no" answers above, how do you intend to correct your money mistake(s)?

   _____

   _____

   _____

3. What are your thoughts, ideas and feelings about the amount of money you deserve?

   _____

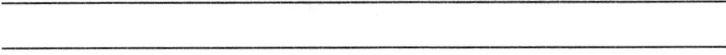

Action Step 3 – Beliefs About Money

In this Action Step you are urged to examine your beliefs about money. Think about these questions very carefully and answer them as best you can.

1. Do you think money is bad or wrong? Why?

   _____

   _____

   _____

2. Do you believe that money makes you powerful and without money you are weak? Why?

   _____

   _____

   _____

3. Do you believe that there is a shortage of money? Why?

   _____

   _____

   _____

4. Do you deserve more money? Why?

   _____

   _____

   _____

   _____

   _____

   _____

   _____

   _____

   _____

5. Now, answer the following question: What *should* your beliefs be about money in these areas?

    _____

    _____

    _____

6. What are your thoughts, ideas and feelings about your beliefs concerning money?

    _____

    _____

    _____

    _____

    _____

    _____

    _____

    _____

    _____

    _____

    _____

    _____

    _____

    _____

    _____

    _____

    _____

    _____

    _____

    _____

    _____

Action Step 4 –Develop A Plan

In this Action Step it is time for you to start thinking about a plan of action to improve your financial situation. Ask yourself the following questions:

1. Do you have an effective plan for bringing more money into your life?

_____

_____

_____

2. If not, why not?

_____

_____

_____

3. If so, what is it?

_____

_____

_____

4. What are your thoughts, ideas and feelings about developing and maintaining a plan of action for your finances?

_____

_____

_____

Action Step 5 ~ Part 1 – Honest Work

In part 1 of this Action Step you will be examining your work habits to see if they meet the standard of honest work. Answer these questions:

1. Are you doing honest work, if not why not?

   _____

   _____

   _____

2. What actions or activities do you do when you are working that you shouldn't? Do you leave early, arrive late or take too much time doing other stuff when you should be working?

   _____

   _____

   _____

3. What will you do right now to make sure you are giving your work the attention that it needs?

   _____

   _____

   _____

4. If you would like to take this activity one step further, sit down with someone you report to, if possible, to answer these questions about you.

   _____

   _____

   _____

5. What are your thoughts, ideas and feelings about honest work?

   _____

   _____

   _____

Action Step 5 ~ Part 2 – Smart Work

In part 2 of this Action Step you will be looking at whether you are working smart or not. Ask yourself the following questions:

1. Does your work compliment your health? If not, what can you do to change that?

   _____

   _____

   _____

2. Do you have some type of stake or share in your work?

   _____

   _____

   _____

3. What research can you do today about a business you would be interested in?

   _____

   _____

   _____

4. How do you get the important people in your life involved?

   _____

   _____

   _____

5. What are your thoughts, ideas and feelings about smart work?

   _____

   _____

   _____

Action Step 5 - Part 3 - Fulfilling Work

In part 3 of this Action Step you will uncover what you really want to do and begin looking for ways to make money doing it. Ask yourself the following questions:

1. Are you doing work that you love? If not, why not?

2. What do you love to do?

3. How can you make money doing it?

4. What is one action you can take today to move yourself closer to doing work you love?

5. What are your thoughts, ideas and feelings about fulfilling work?

Action Step 5 ~ Part 4 – Moderate Work

In part 4 of this Action Step you will examine your work habits to see if you are working in moderation or overworking yourself and therefore damaging other areas of your life. Ask yourself the following questions:

1. How much time do you spend working in proportion to the rest of your life?

_____
_____
_____

2. Is working too much damaging other areas of your life? How?

_____
_____
_____

3. What areas of your life can be improved if you begin working in moderation? How?

_____
_____
_____

4. What actions will you take in order to make sure you are not overworking?

_____
_____
_____

5. What are your thoughts, ideas and feelings about moderate work?

_____
_____
_____

Action Step 6 – Tithing

In this Action Step you are going to begin tithing. Do the following activities:

1. How often do you make money (weekly, monthly, etc.)?

_____

_____

_____

2. How much do you make?

_____

_____

_____

3. What is ten percent of that?

_____

_____

_____

4. Will you give your full ten percent? When?

_____

_____

_____

5. What are your thoughts, ideas and feelings about tithing?

_____

_____

_____

Action Step 7 – Grateful Receiving

In this Action Step you are going to start the process of leaning to gratefully receive. Do the following activities:

1. Why do you deserve to have abundance in your life?

   _____
   _____
   _____

2. Do you allow yourself to gratefully receive? How?

   _____
   _____
   _____

3. What are you doing to become a better steward of the resources you have been trusted with?

   _____
   _____
   _____

4. Who have you allowed to give to you today?

   _____
   _____
   _____

5. Log your success, what are your thoughts, ideas and feelings about grateful receiving?

   _____
   _____
   _____

Action Step 8 – Saving/Investing

In this Action Step you are going to examine your saving and investing habits and develop a plan to improve them. Answer the following questions:

1. Are you saving 10% of your income? If not, why not?

   _____

   _____

   _____

2. What did you buy recently that you probably shouldn't have?

   _____

   _____

   _____

3. What can you do to make sure you are saving/investing more?

   _____

   _____

   _____

4. What is your saving and investment objective for the next 12 months?

   _____

   _____

   _____

5. Log your success, what are your thoughts, ideas and feeling about saving and investing?

   _____

   _____

   _____

Action Step 9 – Eliminating Debt

In this Action Step you are going to examine your current debt situation and begin taking steps to get yourself to stop relying on credit cards and loans to live. Answer the following questions about your debt situation:

1. What do you normally buy on credit that you can eliminate?

    _____

    _____

    _____

2. How much more do you commit to paying on your existing credit cards or loans each month?

    _____

    _____

    _____

3. When will you create a budget? What tools will you use?

    _____

    _____

    _____

4. How much will you put aside in your emergency fund every week, month, etc? Where will this money come from?

    _____

    _____

    _____

5. Log your success, what are your thoughts, ideas and feelings about your level of debt and how you plan to eliminate it?

    _____

    _____

    _____

Action Step 10 – Make Wise Decisions

In this Action Step, you are going to begin making wise decisions when it comes to your money. Answer the following questions to complete your activities for making wise decisions:

1. What do you know about saving and investing? What do you need to learn?

    _____

    _____

    _____

2. Is there a decision that you have been putting off about your finances? If so, what is it? What is your decision?

    _____

    _____

    _____

3. Who do you know that is successful in their finances and when will you speak to them?

    _____

    _____

    _____

4. What are your current limiting beliefs about money and what will you change them to?

    _____

    _____

    _____

5. Log your success. What are your thoughts, ideas and feelings about making wise decisions with your money?

    _____

    _____

    _____

Action Step 11 – Part 1 – Material Possessions

In part 1 of this Action Step, it is time to examine your relationship with material possessions. Answer the following questions as they relate to money and your "stuff:"

1. Have you made the pursuit of money and material possessions your life's focus? What is your primary reason for existence?

    _____

    _____

    _____

2. What do you treasure most? Why?

    _____

    _____

    _____

3. Where does God rank on your 5 most important priorities?

    _____

    _____

    _____

4. Write a statement about your value as a person regardless of how much money you make or what you own.

    _____

    _____

    _____

5. Log your success, what are your thoughts, ideas and feelings about your material possessions?

    _____

    _____

    _____

Action Step 11 - Part 2 - Being Content

In part 2 of this Action Step, you are going to be taking a look at your present level of contentment. Answer the following questions as they relate to money and your "stuff:"

1. What is important to you? Where does money rank in importance?

   _____

   _____

   _____

2. What are you doing to meet your spiritual needs?

   _____

   _____

   _____

3. How can you stay focused on your own improvement in your finances without comparing yourself to others?

   _____

   _____

   _____

4. What are you grateful for in your life? How can you show this gratitude?

   _____

   _____

   _____

5. Log your success, what are your thoughts, ideas and feelings about being content?

   _____

   _____

   _____

Action Step 12 – Part 1 – Weathering Storms

In this Action Step, you will be preparing yourself to get through the financial storms that will come. Here is an activity for you:

1. Do you have quotes and scriptures prepared in advance for when you encounter a financial storm? If so, what are they? If not then do that now.

_____

_____

_____

2. What are some things you can do without if you need to?

_____

_____

_____

3. What are you doing to increase your wisdom in your financial decisions?

_____

_____

_____

4. Are you praying about your money and finances? If not, why not?

_____

_____

_____

5. Log your success, what are your thoughts, ideas and feelings about weathering financial storms

_____

_____

_____

Action Step 12 ~ Part 2 ~ God Reliance

In this Action Step, you are going to start relying more on God and less on yourself for your money and finances. Do the following activities to see where you are in trusting God with your finances:

1. What abilities has God given you to produce wealth?

   _____
   _____
   _____

2. What are you doing to become more God reliant and less self-reliant in your finances?

   _____
   _____
   _____

3. Are you responsible enough to be blessed? How so?

   _____
   _____
   _____

4. Why are you seeking more wealth?

   _____
   _____
   _____

5. Log your success, what are your thoughts, ideas and feelings about being reliant on God?

   _____
   _____
   _____

References

1 Proverbs 21:21 (NIV)

2 Proverbs 23:4 (NIV)

3 Philippians 4:12 (NIV)

4 to read more about Paul please refer to Acts 8-9 in The Bible:

5 Dale Carnegie (writer, lecturer 1888-1955)

6 Proverbs 19:20 (NIV)

7 Psalm 128 (MSG)

8 Philippians 4:7 (NIV)

9 Proverbs 20:18 (NIV)

10 I do not recommend that you change your own brakes unless you completely understand how and have all the appropriate tools.

11 1 Thessalonians 5:17 (NIV)

12 Author Unknown.

13 Proverbs 27:6 (ESV)

14 Dale Carnegie (Writer and lecturer, 1888-1955)

15 Anonymous

16 Ephesians 4:32 (NIV)

17 Anonymous

18 Matthew 5:43-44 (NIV)

19 Ephesians 4:25-26 (NIV)

20 Proverbs 29:20 (NIV)

21 Exodus 20:5 (NIV)

22 Deuteronomy 24:15 (NIV)

23 David Seabury (American Psychologist, Author, 1885-1960)

24 Leviticus 26:40-42 (NIV)

25 Exodus 20:6 (NIV)

26 Numbers 14:18 (NIV)

27 Deuteronomy 10:19 (NIV)

28 Proverbs 22:6 (NIV)

29 Matthew 18:26 (NIV)

30 Galatians 5:22-23 (NIV)

31 Proverbs 29:15 & 17 (MSG)

32 Norman Vincent Peale (Minister and Author, 1898-1993)

33 Philippians 4:6-8 (NIV)

34 Dale Carnegie (Writer and lecturer, 1888-1955)

35 2 Corinthians 9:6-8 (NIV)

36 1 Corinthians 7:3-4 (NIV)

37 Dale Carnegie (Writer and lecturer, 1888-1955)

38 John Wesley (Angelican clergyman, 1703-1791)

39 Deuteronomy 15:10 (NIV)

40 Galatians 6:8 (MSG)

41 Winston Churchill (British statesman, Prime Minister 1874-1965)

42 Mother Teresa (Christian Missionary, 1910-1997)

43 Matthew 6:19-21 (NIV)

44 Proverbs 11:24-25 (MSG)

45 2 Corinthians 9:6-8 (NIV)

46 Mark 16:15 (NIV)

47 Romans 3:23 (NIV)

48 Luke 19:10 (MSG)

49 Romans 10:1-(NIV)

50 Romans 15:1-2 (MSG)

51 1 Peter 2:9 (MSG)

52 Hebrews 5:12 (NIV)

53 Matthew 5:11-12 (NIV)

54 Galatians 1:10 (NIV)

55 Romans 6:23 (NIV)

56 Philippians 4:13 (NIV)

57 Luke 8:14 (NIV)

58 1John 2:15-17 (NIV)

59 Luke 16:13 (NIV)

60 Matthew 28:19 (NIV)

61 Romans 13:8 (NIV)

62 Luke 15:7 (MSG)

63 1 Thessalonians 2:19-20 (MSG)

64 Galatians 6:7-10 (NIV)

65 Psalm 112:5 (NIV)

66 Galatians 6:7 (KJV)

67 Proverbs 28:27 (NIV)

68 See Galatians 6:9 (NIV)

69 Norman Cousins (Journalist, author 1915-1990)

70 Albert Einstein (Swiss Physicist, 1879-1955)

71 Malachi 3:10 (NIV)

72 I Timothy 6:10 (NIV)

73 Luke 6:30-32 & 36-38 (NIV)

74 Edith Wharton (American writer, 1862-1937)

75 Luke 6:32-35 (NIV)

76 Psalm 37:21 (NIV)

77 Elizabeth Harrison (American Educator, 1849-1927)

78 Samuel Taylor (English Poet, philosopher, 1772-1834)

79 Galatians 6:9 (NIV)

80 The Babylonian Talmud

81 Matthew 12:33 (MSG)

82 3 John 1:2 (NIV)

83 Plato (Greek Philosopher, 428-347 bc)

84 Edward Stanley (Earl of Derby, 1826-1893)

85 1 Timothy 4:8 (NIV)

86 Author Unknown

87 Parents Magazine- September 2009 - pg. 94

88 Parents Magazine September 2009 page 94.

89 Parents Magazine – September 2009, pg. 96

90 Proverbs 23:1-3 (NIV)

91 Deuteronomy 8:10 (NIV)

92 Proverbs 23:29-35 (NIV)

93 Personal Power 2 – Anthony Robbins (Motivational Speaker, 1960-Present)

94 Author Unknown

95 1 Corinthians 6:19-20 (NIV)

96 Romans 12:3 (NIV)

97 Proverbs 17:22 (MSG)

98 Jeremiah 12:5 (NIV)

99 Hebrews 12:12-13 (MSG)

100 1 Timothy 6:10 (KJV)

101 Anonymous (The Language of Letting go, Melody Beattie pg. 326)

102 1 Timothy 6:10 (NIV)

103 Ecclesiastes 5:10 (NIV)

104 Ayn Rand (Russian born American Writer and Novelist 1905-1982)

105 2 Thessalonians 3:10 (NIV)

106 Genesis 2:15 (NIV)

107 Ecclesiastes 9:10 (NIV)

108 Proverbs 14:23 (NIV)

109 Proverbs 21:5 (NIV)

110 Henry Ford (Industrialist & Inventor 1863-1947)

111 Andrew Carnegie (American Industrialist 1835-1919)

112 Proverbs 18:9 (NIV)

113 Ecclesiastes 2:24-25 (NIV)

114 Exodus 23:12 (NIV)

115 Ecclesiastes 5:12 (NIV)

116 Ecclesiastes 5:3 (MSG)

117 Psalm 128:2 (NIV)

118 Louisa May Alcott (American Author 1832-1888)

119 1 Thessalonians 4:11-12 (NIV)

120 Proverbs 3:9-10 (NIV)

121 Statistics from Barna Research

122 Malachi 3:10 (NIV)

123 Selwyn Hughes (Welsh Christian Minister 1928-2006)

124 Luke 6:38 (NIV)

125 Mark 12:41-44 (NIV)

126 2 Corinthians 9:7 (NIV)

127 Mark 4:24 (MSG)

128 Billy Graham, (Evangelist 1918-Present)

129 Galatians 6:7 (NIV)

130 Acts 20:35 (NIV)

131 Henry David Thoreau (Author 1817-1862)

132 Benjamin Franklin (American Inventor, Statesmen and printer 1706-1790)

133 Proverbs 21:20 (NLT)

134 As of 2011

135 Ecclesiastes 11:2 (NLT)

136 Proverbs 22:7 (NIV)

137 Flip Wilson, American Comedian (1893-1998)

138 Publitius Syrus (Roman Author 1st Century BC)

139 Benjamin Franklin (American Inventor, Statesmen and printer 1706-1790)

140 Henry Wheeler Shaw (Politician/Humorist 1818-1885)

141 Andrew Jackson (17th President of the United States 1767-1845)

142 Deuteronomy 15:6 (NIV)

143 Matthew 25: 14-30 (NIV)

144 Dave Ramsey (Author 1960-Present)

145 Proverbs 24:3-4 (NIV)

146 Proverbs 27:12 (NIV)

147 Luke 16:10-12 (NIV)

148 James W. Frick (Author 1923-2008)

149 Matthew 6:21 - (NIV)

150 Proverbs 28:20 - (NIV)

151 1 Timothy 6:10 - (NIV)

152 Benjamin Franklin (American Inventor, Statesmen and printer 1706-1790)

153 Robert A. Savage, Former President & CEO American Express (1933-Present)

154 Matthew 4:4 (NIV)

155 Benjamin Franklin (American Inventor, Statesmen and printer 1706-1790)

156 Matthew 20:1-13 (NIV)

157 Matthew 20:13 (NIV)

158 Franklin D. Roosevelt (32nd President of the United States 1882-1945)

159 Hebrews 13:5 (NKJV)

160 Ecclesiastes 7:12 (NIV)

161 Philippians 4:12-13 (NIV)

162 Thomas Jefferson (3rd President of the United States 1743-1826)

163 Proverbs 28:22 (NLT)

164 Thomas Dekker (Writer 1572-1632)

165 Proverbs 11:24-25 (NIV)

166 Deuteronomy 8:18 (NIV)

167 Mark 10:29-30 (NIV)

168 Romans 8:31-32 (NIV)

169 Timothy 6:11 (NIV)

170 Matthew 6:33 (KJV)

www.ingramcontent.com/pod-product-compliance
Lightning Source LLC
Chambersburg PA
CBHW051944090426
42741CB00008B/1263